30-SECOND
TWENTIETH
CENTURY

30-SECOND
TWENTIETH CENTURY

The 50 most significant ideas and events, each explained in half a minute

Editor
Jonathan T. Reynolds

Contributors
Grace Chee
Caryn Connelly
Candice Goucher
Cary D. Harlow
Kristin Hornsby
Laura J. Lee
Craig A. Lockard
Sara Patenaude
Jonathan T. Reynolds
Jeremy Rich
Timothy D. Sofranko
Kristopher Teters
Rita R. Thomas
Russell Zimmerman

METRO BOOKS
New York

METRO BOOK
New York

An Imprint of Sterling Publishing
1166 Avenue of the Americas
New York, NY 10036

This book was conceived,
designed, and produced by

Ivy Press
210 High Street, Lewes,
East Sussex BN7 2NS, U.K.
www.ivypress.co.uk

Creative Director **Peter Bridgewater**
Publisher **Susan Kelly**
Editorial Director **Tom Kitch**
Art Director **Michael Whitehead**
Editor **Jamie Pumfrey**
Designer **Ginny Zeal**
Illustrator **Ivan Hissey**
Glossaries Text **Jonathan T. Reynolds**

ISBN-13: 978-1-4351-6086-6

For information about custom
editions, special sales, and premium
and corporate purchases, please contact
Sterling Special Sales at 800-805-5489
or specialsales@sterlingpublishing.com.

Manufactured in China

Color origination by Ivy Press Reprographics

2 4 6 8 10 9 7 5 3 1

www.sterlingpublishing.com

CONTENTS

INTRODUCTION:
A CENTURY OF CONTRADICTIONS
Jonathan T. Reynolds

Perhaps no era in human history has seen such a transformation of the human condition as the 20th century. Those hundred years witnessed a host of breakthrough technologies in transportation (to the Moon and back!) and communication, from recording of sound on 78s to the speed of the Internet, and extraordinary advances in medicine and science, including the discovery of the structure of DNA—the very stuff of life. Socially and politically, the 20th century is also remembered for shifts toward gender and racial equality with its movements for women's rights, civil rights, decolonization, and the end of apartheid. As such, the century is often presented as predominantly positive—breaking down the barriers of time and space separating human communities and curing previously deadly or debilitating diseases. Indeed, it has often been heralded as a period of progress.

Both sides of the coin
However, the last century also had a dark side. While some technologies and social innovations could improve or extend human life, others were likely to result in the opposite. New, more deadly weapons, from poison gas to nuclear bombs, were joined with long-range delivery systems to expand radically a country's ability to kill its enemy. All too often, politics and ideology seemed to outweigh humanity. Such developments blurred the line between soldiers and civilians as those out of uniform were targeted to brutal effect. Similarly, even as a growing concept of human rights sought to protect individual liberties, new political systems such as fascism sought to subvert the rights of the individual to those of the state—and to deny similar rights to others.

Metaphorically, one might think of the 20th century as a toolbox to which items were constantly being added, some of which could be used to help people, and others to cause harm. With ever-increasing globalization the 20th century finally triumphed over smallpox while experiencing rapidly spreading pandemics. It saw the development of

Man on the moon
20th-century progress allowed for humanity to begin exploring the world outside our atmosphere.

powered flight, and the dropping of a nuclear weapon from an aircraft. From world wars to Woodstock, the last century expresses the human condition from every conceivable angle.

How the book works

In order to understand the complex legacy bequeathed to us by the 20th century, this book seeks to present those hundred tumultuous years through a few dozen carefully selected events, issues, and personalities. Fifty 30-second histories, each written by a scholar from a relevant academic field, are divided into seven thematic categories in order to present the global breadth of the human experience. Each one is presented consistently, in just 300 words, delivered as: a single main paragraph that sets out the topic in detail; a "3-second Thrash," summing up the event in one sentence; and a second, shorter paragraph, the "3-minute Thought," offering further insight and broader context. Key terms are defined in a glossary within each section and each has a profile of an individual whose life and work embodied the issues and events included under the theme.

The first, **Science & Technology**, brings together some of the most remarkable discoveries and inventions that changed the way we live, from advances in agriculture to exploration of space. Section two, **Arts & Entertainment**, celebrates the cultural events that brightened our world through music, dance, paintings, and play. Against the century's backdrop of progress and enhancement were world wars, fights for freedom, and ideological struggles. Those conflicts and sacrifices—global, national, and personal—are recorded in the following two sections: **War & Conflicts** and **Politics & Society**. Individuals stand out for their dreams and ideas in the next section, **Industry & Economics**, from Kwame Nkrumah to Joseph Stalin to Henry Ford. The two final sections, **Medicine & Health** and **Events, Triumphs & Disasters**, record the best and worst of human endeavor, from the eradication of smallpox to the darkest period in living memory: the Holocaust. No doubt some of the subjects chosen will be familiar to you, but we hope that *30-Second Twentieth Century* will surprise you with a few unfamiliar topics, personalities, and perspectives as well.

We are all born into history. It is not unlike turning on a movie rather late into the story. Unless you learn what it is that you missed, the part you are watching is unlikely to make much sense at all. It is our profound wish that this volume not only enriches your understanding of the 20th century, but also of the world in which we live today.

Jonathan T. Reynolds
Northern Kentucky University, 2014

Devastating consequences
Human innovation was also responsible for some of the most traumatic events in the 20th century; the advancement in atomic energy resulted in the bombings of Hiroshima and Nagasaki.

SCIENCE & TECHNOLOGY

SCIENCE & TECHNOLOGY
GLOSSARY

1991 Gore Bill Officially titled the High Performance Computing Act of 1991, this legislation was proposed by then Senator Al Gore. The initiative provided incentives for an expansion of Internet capacity and penetration, and also helped fund Mosaic, the first browser that allowed individuals to search and connect to other computer data on the Internet.

Advanced Research Projects Agency
Established in 1958, ARPA was established to facilitate research into defensive technologies as part of the Cold War competition between the United States and Soviet Union. In 1972 the term Defense was added to the name (DARPA). Among the most significant developments were Arpanet (see below) and the satellite positioning system known as GPS.

ARPANET In response to the fear that a nuclear attack on the US would disable existing systems of communication, ARPA was tasked with developing a packet-based network of computers to facilitate high-speed and secure messages. The success of ARPANET helped lay the foundation for the Internet and the World Wide Web.

Geiger-Marsden Experiment Also known as the Rutherford gold foil experiments. These investigations into the nature of atomic structure took place from 1908 to 1913 at the University of Manchester, UK. By examining how protons and neutrons impacted gold foil, researchers at the University of Manchester were able to establish that atoms were comprised of a nucleus composed of protons and neutrons and orbited by electrons.

The Manhattan Project In 1939, the United States launched a top-secret research program to investigate the potential of atomic weapons. By 1942, in cooperation with the British and Canadians, the project was well under way. By 1945 the project had succeeded in producing the Trinity test bomb and the weapons used against Nagasaki and Hiroshima. In so doing, they launched the Atomic Age and set the stage for the Cold War.

Syncom 3 Launched in 1964, Syncom 3 was the first geostationary communications satellite. Stationed above the International Date Line over the Pacific Ocean, the satellite was used to provide coverage of the Tokyo Summer Olympics to North America.

Transmission Control Protocol/Internet Protocol (TCP/IP) This is the system adopted by ARPA in the 1960s to regulate how data was transmitted, received, and confirmed within a computer network. The system was adopted by the US Department of Defense in 1982. In the 1990s, it would become the standard for regulating the flow of information in the Internet and World Wide Web.

THE THEORY OF RELATIVITY

the 30-second history

Relativity is one of the pillars of modern physics and key to understanding how the world works, from your GPS to an atomic clock. Formulated in two theories, Albert Einstein's ideas about special and general relativity have been described as among the biggest leaps of the scientific imagination in world history. Using a 1919 solar eclipse, Einstein predicted that light rays from distant stars were deflected by the gravity pull of the Sun. This observation, together with his earlier (1915) theory that distance and time are not absolute (but are affected by motion and gravity), allowed Einstein to propose the first revolutionary theory since Isaac Newton, some 250 years before. It all began with $e = mc^2$, or "energy equals mass times the speed of light squared," the famous mathematical equation that Einstein argued explained the laws of Nature. The idea that energy and matter were one and the same is behind the Big Bang theory of the beginning of the Universe, the theory of black holes, the nuclear world, and countless other processes in the Universe.

3-SECOND THRASH
The theory of relativity (1919) that made Albert Einstein the rock star of science leaped light years ahead to the field of quantum physics.

3-MINUTE THOUGHT
In 2010, scientists at CERN (the European Organization for Nuclear Research) conducted an experiment in which neutrinos (subatomic particles) appeared to be traveling faster than the speed of light. If this were true, then the age of the universe and the theories of modern physics were out the window. For once, scientists were hoping to be wrong—and they were. The rest of us were able to see scientific method at work. Einstein, who said, "the important thing is not to stop questioning," might have been pleased.

RELATED TOPICS
See also
SPLITTING THE ATOM
page 16

ALBERT EINSTEIN
page 20

HIROSHIMA
page 62

"ONE GIANT LEAP"
page 148

3-SECOND BIOGRAPHIES
ISAAC NEWTON
1643–1727
English physicist, whose theory of gravity started the Scientific Revolution

ALBERT EINSTEIN
1879–1955
German physicist who won the Nobel Prize in 1921 for his explanation of the photoelectric effect

30-SECOND TEXT
Candice Goucher

Einstein theorized that because the Sun is so heavy, its gravity field should deflect light by a measurable amount.

SPLITTING THE ATOM

the 30-second history

Before Ernest Rutherford's experiments in 1909, scientists could only speculate as to the shape of atoms, believed at the time to be the smallest particles on Earth. Rutherford was the first to prove that atoms consist of a tightly packed nucleus and orbiting electrons, "subatomic particles." In 1917 Rutherford led another experiment to study nuclear transmutation, or the changing atoms of one element into atoms of another. He was able to change nitrogen atoms into oxygen—the first example of scientists causing a nuclear reaction, or "splitting the atom." In 1932, expanding on Rutherford's work, Ernest Walton and John Cockcroft split a lithium-7 nucleus into two. When German scientists attempted nuclear fission on heavier elements, including uranium, they discovered that the process of fission created huge bursts of energy. Subsequent experiments on nuclear chain reactions during the Second World War caught the eye of both United States and German government officials, who poured money into research on using nuclear fission to aid the war effort. America's Manhattan Project completed the creation of the first atomic bombs in 1945. Peaceful generation of nuclear power began in 1954 with the Soviet Union Obninsk power station.

3-SECOND THRASH
Ernest Rutherford discovered that atomic nuclei were not a solid, unbreakable mass, but could be purposely split apart in a nuclear reaction.

3-MINUTE THOUGHT
The first atomic bombs (A-Bombs) worked through nuclear fission, or breaking apart the nucleus of atoms. Hydrogen bombs (H-Bombs) add on a process of nuclear fusion, forcing two or more nuclei to fuse together. H-bombs are thermonuclear weapons, which use the heat created by a nuclear fission bomb to ignite nuclear fusion, giving the bombs even more destructive power. Virtually all modern nuclear weapons use thermonuclear technology.

RELATED TOPICS
See also
HIROSHIMA
page 62

THE CUBAN MISSILE CRISIS
page 82

3-SECOND BIOGRAPHIES
ERNEST RUTHERFORD
1871–1937
British physicist, awarded the Nobel Prize in Chemistry in 1908

JOHN COCKCROFT
1897–1967
British physicist, awarded the Nobel Prize in Physics in 1951 alongside Ernest Walton

ERNEST WALTON
1903–95
Irish physicist, awarded the Nobel Prize in Physics in 1951 alongside John Cockcroft

30-SECOND TEXT
Sara Patenaude

Ernest Rutherford's proof that the atom could be split into smaller parts paved the way for atomic bombs and nuclear power.

$^{235}_{92}U$

$^{92}_{36}Kr$

$^{236}_{92}U$

$^{141}_{56}Ba$

THE GREEN REVOLUTION

the 30-second history

Although the label "Green Revolution" might bring to mind a sudden, radical change in environmental policies, it is a term originally coined in 1968 to describe the development of high-yield crops in impoverished countries. As world population grew at increasingly high rates (peaking at 2.2 percent in 1963), the Rockefeller and Ford foundations funded research programs in the 1940s aimed at increasing wheat production in Mexico. Through 20 years of specialized breeding, new strains were developed that were denser, matured more quickly, and allowed farmers to produce more crops per year than ever before. Other high-yielding varieties (HYVs) of major food crops, including rice, beans, maize, and millet, have been developed and to this day research continues in an attempt to address food shortages in areas that have not yet enjoyed a positive impact from advanced agricultural technologies, notably sub-Saharan Africa. While the Green Revolution has contributed to lower food prices, higher incomes, and improved nutrition in Asia and Latin America, critics argue that these advancements come with a price. Excessive fertilizer and pesticide use, heavy irrigation, and overfarming may result, ultimately, in an even greater hunger crisis for struggling regions.

3-SECOND THRASH
For food supplies to keep pace with Earth's burgeoning population, advanced farming techniques must be developed that adhere to the principle of nonmaleficence ("first, do no harm").

3-MINUTE THOUGHT
The Green Revolution changed commercial crop production, effectively turning countries once synonymous with hunger into some of the world's greatest food producers. However, global hunger remains, and access to resources and patented technologies is an issue for developing nations. Three-quarters of Africa's land is severely depleted and, in response, farmers clear forests and savannas that support wildlife. We must be mindful to include the whole earth in our focus on sustainability.

RELATED TOPICS
See also
SLOPPY PETRI DISH
page 120

ERADICATION OF SMALLPOX
page 128

3-SECOND BIOGRAPHIES
WILLIAM S. GAUD
1907–77
Former Administrator for the US Agency for International Development (USAID) who coined the term "Green Revolution"

NORMAN BORLAUG
1914–2009
American scientist who developed dwarf wheat varieties that transformed agriculture in Mexico, Pakistan, and India: the "Father of the Green Revolution"

30-SECOND TEXT
Laura Lee

Population growth in the 1960s inspired an effort to boost efficiency of crop production in the developing world.

March 14, 1879
Albert Einstein is born to Jewish parents, Hermann and Pauline Einstein, in Ulm, Germany

1884
Young Einstein receives a gift of a compass from his uncle, which sparks his intellectual curiosity

1896
Renounces his German citizenship to avoid service in the German army. For the next four years, Einstein has no legal citizenship in any country

1900
Graduates from the Polytechnic Institute in Zürich with a degree in physics. Begins work on doctorate

1901
Becomes a Swiss citizen

1902
Becomes a father out of wedlock with Mileva Maric. His daughter is put up for adoption. Begins working at the Swiss Patent Office

1903
Marries Mileva Maric. The following year, his son, Hans Albert, is born

1905
Receives his PhD and conceives his equation $E=mc^2$. Publishes five papers this year, including one introducing his general theory of relativity

1909
Appointed extraordinary professor of physics at Zürich University

1910
Second son, Eduard, is born

1919
Divorces Mileva Meric and weds his cousin, Elsa Löwenthal

1921
Receives the Nobel Peace Prize for Physics for his work on the photoelectric effect

1933
Nazi Party comes into power in Germany. Einstein emigrates to the US

1939
Einstein warns US President Roosevelt of the potential of an atomic bomb being created by Germany and urges nuclear research to begin in the US

1940
Manhattan Project begins in the US in an attempt to create an atomic bomb. Einstein becomes a US citizen

1945
US drops two atomic bombs in Japan and the Second World War comes to an end

1948
Supports the creation of the State of Israel and in 1952, is offered the presidency, which he declines

April 18, 1955
Dies of heart failure in New Jersey aged 76

ALBERT EINSTEIN

Albert Einstein, named *Time*
magazine's "Person of the Century" in 1999,
was perhaps the most famous physicist and
thinker of modern times. His wild, white hair
and overgrown moustache make him instantly
recognizable, and his name is synonymous with
"genius." Nobel Prize winner, researcher, and
lecturer, Einstein was also a champion of
frequently unpopular causes, which ultimately
led to an FBI file labeling him an "agitator."

Einstein's early life was spent in Munich.
Contrary to popular belief, he performed quite
well in school. He continued his education at
the prestigious Federal Polytechnic School in
Zürich, training to be a teacher of physics and
mathematics. In time, he held professorships
at the Polytechnic School, the University of
Zürich, the German University of Prague, and
at the Kaiser-Wilhelm-Gesellschaft in Berlin.
From 1933 until his death in 1955, Einstein held
a research position at Princeton University.

Einstein's most famous writings are referred
to as "the 1905 papers," of which three are
particularly notable. The first described
electromagnetic radiation and postulated that
light consisted not only of waves, but also of
discrete particles called photons. Einstein
theorized that a photon's energy could be
determined by multiplying its frequency by a
constant. This work led to his award of a Nobel
Prize in 1921. With his other two papers from
1905, one concerning the special theory of
relativity and the other statistical mechanics,

Einstein importantly contributed to the
knowledge of quantum physics, electromagnetic
radiation, and gravitational acceleration.

With great fame comes conjecture, and it can
be difficult to separate truth from myth. Did he
really wear the same clothes every day? Was he
sociable, or a recluse? One thing we do know
is that Einstein wrote many letters when he
traveled, and those letters (some 1,400 were
released to the public in 2006), indicate quite
a busy love life. While married to his second
wife, Einstein's letters describe a series of
affairs. Whether his wife knew and gave
permission for his trysts is up for speculation.

Einstein was, throughout his life, an
outspoken critic of injustice. He considered
himself a pacifist and spoke out against Hitler's
war efforts. In 1933, he moved permanently to
the United States, and in 1940 became a US
citizen. He reluctantly urged President
Roosevelt to accelerate the country's efforts to
build an atomic bomb after learning that
German scientists had split the uranium atom
and might be working on the development of
an atomic bomb. Einstein later wrote, shortly
before his death, "I made one great mistake
in my life ... when I signed the letter to
President Roosevelt recommending that atom
bombs be made." After his death Einstein
was remembered not only for his scientific
brilliance, but also for his humor, warmth, and
commitment to social responsibility.

Laura J. Lee

TRANSISTOR

the 30-second history

The transistor has been called one of the last century's greatest inventions, and it certainly is one of the most ubiquitous products in use today. Introduced in 1947, it paved the way for the development of smaller, more portable electronic devices. Previously, radios, telephones and televisions depended on fragile glass vacuum tubes to move current in a single direction and increase its flow. These tubes took time to warm up, consumed considerable power, and were bulky and expensive to replace. Transistors work by controlling the amount of electrical current. Operating as an amplifier, a transistor takes a small current and produces a larger one. A transistor can also act as a switch by increasing or decreasing the flow of electrons into or out of a semiconductor (these days, silicon). When positively and negatively charged silicon is layered in different ways, electrons will flow—or not—according to the positioning of contacts. Today's transistors are as small as the diameter of a strand of hair; computer chips may contain a billion transistors! Considering the furniture-sized radios of the pre-transistor era, the invention of the transistor revolutionized the modern electronic age. Further advances in transistor development will result in even faster, smaller, more efficient technology.

RELATED TOPICS
See also
THE WORLD WIDE WEB
page 28

PONG
page 44

3-SECOND THRASH
In an attempt to improve telephone amplification, a team of three physicists created a device that would revolutionize the world of electronics.

3-MINUTE THOUGHT
Three researchers at Bell Labs, New Jersey, one of the world's biggest industrial laboratories, were awarded the 1956 Nobel Prize for their research and conception of the transistor. The first transistor was made by touching gold wire to a crystal of germanium (the semiconductor) and observing the magnified current. With the advent of the transistor, the first portable radio was commercially available in 1954, and a wave of low-cost, mass-produced consumer electronics followed.

3-SECOND BIOGRAPHIES
WALTER BRATTAIN
1902–87
American physicist who shared the 1956 Nobel Prize in Physics

JOHN BARDEEN
1908–91
American physicist and electrical engineer who shared the 1956 Nobel Prize in Physics

WILLIAM SHOCKLEY
1910–89
American physicist and eccentric inventor who shared the 1956 Nobel Prize in Physics

30-SECOND TEXT
Laura J. Lee

Small enough to lose—tiny transistors are getting smaller all the time, making possible iconic products such as the transistor radio and the smartphone.

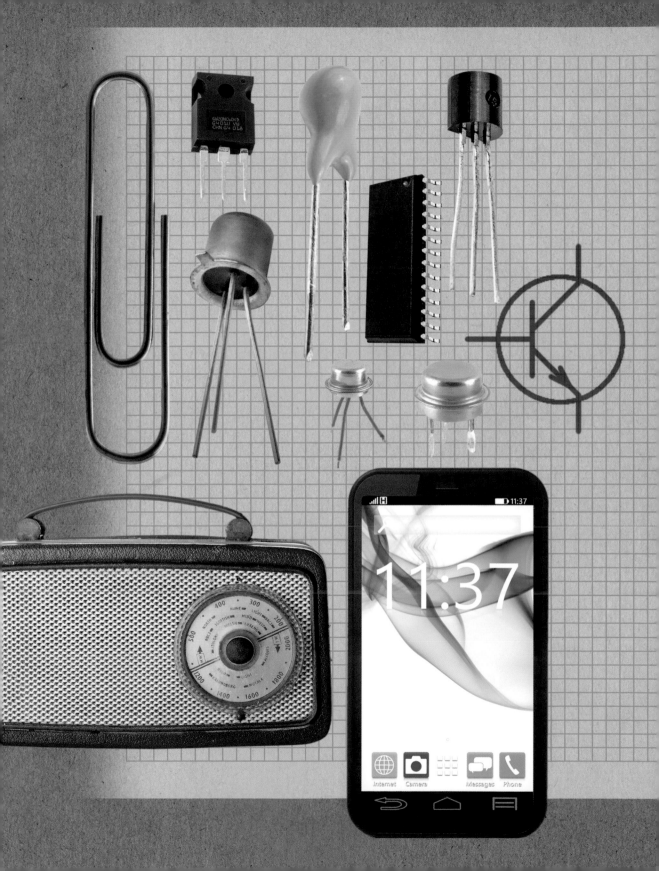

SPUTNIK

the 30-second history

Sputnik 1 was the first manmade satellite launched into Earth's orbit, fired into space by the Soviet Union on October 4, 1957. The Soviets and Americans were locked in the Space Race, eager to upstage one another and claim the Cold War high ground. Project leader Sergei Korolev, once a political prisoner, oversaw the design of a spartan but efficient satellite: *Sputnik 1* was simply a 23in (58cm) polished metal sphere and held only a radio transmitter and thermal measuring instruments, plus a few batteries to power them. *Sputnik 1* was in orbit, regularly emitting a beep, for just 92 days, but it was an accomplishment that shattered the United States' assumptions of its technological superiority. To follow up on the Soviet success, *Sputnik 2* was designed and launched in only a few weeks. It was a larger capsule, cone-shaped, holding an assortment of transmitters and scientific instruments again, but this time also a living creature—a dog, Laika—that became the first animal launched into orbit. Laika lasted only six hours before she died from stress and heat, but the Soviet Union had achieved a second milestone in the Space Race. Combined, the *Sputnik* satellites spent more than 250 days circling the globe.

3-SECOND THRASH
The *Sputnik* program was a pair of satellites launched late in 1957, when the Soviet Union took the lead in the Space Race.

3-MINUTE THOUGHT
The Space Race was a battle between scientists but also part of a larger political and often military contest. As the Second World War had seen German rocket attacks against Britain and also the American deployment of atomic weapons against Japan, rocket technology represented a very real means of projecting force. The idea that "*Sputnik* is watching you" was hardly comforting to those in the West, and for many this Soviet success was cause for concern, not celebration.

RELATED TOPIC
See also
SPLITTING THE ATOM
page 16

3-SECOND BIOGRAPHIES
SERGEI KOROLEV
1907–66
Soviet rocket scientist and lead engineer on the *Sputnik* program, formally known as "Chief Designer"

WERNHER VON BRAUN
1912–77
German engineer and rocket scientist, icon of the American space program following his post-Second World War recruitment

KERIM KERIMOV
1917–2003
Azerbaijani/Soviet rocket scientist and a pivotal figure in the Soviet space program

30-SECOND TEXT
Russell Zimmerman

The Soviet Union made the most of its victory over the US in the Space Race by issuing stamps featuring Laika and the Sputnik satellites.

SHQIPERIA
LAIKA 1

4 октября
1957
40
ПОЧТА СССР

10в

20전

Sputnik 1 1957

GLOBAL BROADCAST OF "ALL YOU NEED IS LOVE"

the 30-second history

For almost all of human history distance demanded that human communication be limited to those within earshot. Development of telegraphy in the 18th and 19th centuries launched the human conquest of immediate communication over large distances. By the 20th century the growth of commercial radio and television began to enable mass transmission of information and entertainment to wide audiences. Not until the 1964 launch of the first geostationary satellite, Syncom 3, however, did regular transcontinental live broadcasts become feasible. Conceived in 1966, the *Our World* global simulcast required some 10,000 technicians and the use of four satellites and coordinated broadcasts to 31 countries in 22 languages. Features on Pablo Picasso and Maria Callas combined with scenes from the Tokyo subway. The climax of the two-and-a-half-hour program was a performance by the Beatles of a never-before-heard song, written especially to celebrate love and peace. Unfortunately, plans to include the Soviet Union and eastern bloc states in the program ended barely a week before the scheduled broadcast, when the Soviet Union and its allies withdrew in protest over Western support of Israel in the 1967 Arab-Israeli war. Politics, once again, proved able to thwart the effort to unite people.

3-SECOND THRASH
On June 25, 1967 some 700 million people around the world turned on their televisions to watch the Beatles perform "All You Need Is Love."

3-MINUTE THOUGHT
While television had become common in most countries around the world by the mid-1960s, live broadcasts were limited in range due to the challenge of sending signals around the curvature of the Earth. By coordinating a series of geostationary communication satellites, the British program *Our World* was able to achieve the first international live television broadcast although its bid to ease Cold War tensions by uniting a divided world failed.

RELATED TOPICS
See also
TRANSISTOR
page 22

SPUTNIK
page 24

THE WORLD WIDE WEB
page 28

THE FIRST ARAB-ISRAELI WAR
page 64

3-SECOND BIOGRAPHIES
HERMAN POTOCNIK
1892–1929
Slovenian scientist who first proposed the utility of geostationary satellites for communication

ARTHUR C. CLARKE
1917–2008
British science fiction author who popularized the idea of the geostationary communications satellite

30-SECOND TEXT
Jonathan T. Reynolds

Satellites transmitted the Beatles' message about the power of love, but Cold War tensions limited their reach.

THE WORLD WIDE WEB

the 30-second history

The Internet emerged during the Cold War, funded by a tiny fraction of taxpayers' trillions spent on defense. In 1957, the US Department of Defense's Advanced Research Projects Agency (ARPA) launched "resource sharing," a project to connect university and military computers across the country for the space program. Arpanet, the Internet's precursor, began on October 29, 1969 as the first message ("lo," for login) sent from the University of California to Stanford. "Networking" took a revolutionary step with evolving email software and the @ symbol, transforming communication and data sharing. By 1975, Arpanet was operational, with 75 linked university and military computers. The Internet as we know it arrived in 1983, when 14 separate networks from private and public spheres interfaced via a single international language, Transmission Control Protocol/Internet Protocol (TCP/IP). In 1989 Tim Berners-Lee invented a user-friendly system to categorize and collect information, naming it the World Wide Web. By the late 1980s, some 200,000 computers accessed more than 400 networks. The 1991 Gore Bill eased the exponentially growing web traffic by constructing Network Access Points (NAPs). Allowing billions of users to become linked, the one web became vast: open, accessible, changing, and evolving.

3-SECOND THRASH
An unintended accomplishment of Cold War space competition, the web links human users, computers, and networks worldwide, providing instant access to one virtual world.

3-MINUTE THOUGHT
Three major revolutions have changed societies on a grand scale: the agricultural, industrial, and the Internet revolutions. Previously the stuff of sci-fi, the web has completely transformed the everyday lives of ordinary people, leveling the field in commerce, education, entertainment, media, politics, and social networking. The free, neutral net links human individuals instantaneously, rendering geographical boundaries, political borders, and class status nearly irrelevant.

RELATED TOPICS
See also
"ONE GIANT LEAP"
page 148

THE FALL OF THE
BERLIN WALL
page 150

3-SECOND BIOGRAPHIES
Leonard Kleinrock
1934–
American engineer and professor, who invented the "packet" system of sending information. His student sent the first internet message from UCLA to Stanford in 1969

RAYMOND TOMLINSON
1941–
American programmer who wrote a better code for email and invented the @ sign

AL GORE
1948–
American Senator who backed legislation creating web super highways to ease traffic

30-SECOND TEXT
Grace Chee

Any connected individual can reach out via the web right across the world.

ARTS & ENTERTAINMENT

ARTS & ENTERTAINMENT
GLOSSARY

78s/78rpm Because of their ease of manufacture, transport, and storage, 78rpm vinyl records (which rotated 78 times per minute) became the dominant form of musical reproduction during the 1930s. Each side of the disc could hold roughly three minutes of recorded music.

Cubism Cubism was among the most striking components of artistic Modernism. Artists such as Pablo Picasso and Georges Braque utilized the style to break up, analyze, and represent a subject from a variety of perspectives at a single time. While Picasso is often credited with the creation of the technique, many scholars argue that he was himself influenced by existing artwork from parts of Africa and Austronesia that featured similar stylistic elements.

Gosateizm One of the core intellectual components of Marxist-Leninist Communism as practiced in the Soviet Union was gosateizm, or official state atheism. As such, the Soviet Union rejected all forms of religious belief and tolerated only closely regulated religious practice.

Modernism An intellectual and artistic movement, Modernism began in the late 19th century as thinkers, painters, architects, musicians, and others began to reject the conventions and orthodoxies of their fields. For example, painters rejected realistic depictions and composers broke with musical convention by embracing elements such as syncopation and atonality. The embrace of secularism was an important component of intellectual Modernism.

Phonograph Building on the advent of recording technologies in the late 1800s, by the 1920s and 1930s record players were becoming common around the world. For the first time, music ceased to be a local and fleeting experience, and became something that could be reproduced, transported, and enjoyed repeatedly. The result was a global exchange of musical cultures such as the world had never before experienced.

Rumba A variant of the Cuban Spanish term for "party" (*rumbo*), this term developed to describe an Afro-Cuban musical style popular at secular dance parties. African elements of syncopation and polyrhythm (two or more rythms at once) were central to the music's sound and energy. A global Rumba Craze in the 1930s helped spread these musical elements around the world

Syncopation A core Modernist component of music, syncopation introduced musical rhythms wherein performers would intentionally play "off beat" by "swinging" the notes or overlapping and juxtaposing two or more time signatures in a polyrhythmic manner. Syncopation was a feature of much African music, and the influence spread from jazz, blues, and gospel eventually to transform the composition and performance of other styles of music, ranging from classical to bluegrass.

LES DEMOISELLES D'AVIGNON

the 30-second history

Revolutionary, innovative, and controversial, Picasso's *Demoiselles* marks the rise of Modernism and Cubism—a major Modernist style. The European Modernist movement was a cultural revolution that shaped new expressions in art, architecture, music, dance, literature, and science in the 20th century. Modern artists resisted tradition, departing from representations of reality and experimenting with distortions of form and emotional, abstract, multidimensional perspectives. Many, including Picasso, found inspiration in West African art. Partially influenced by the nudes of Cézanne, Matisse, and others, *Demoiselles* anticipated Picasso's emerging Cubist style. He depicts five nude women in a Barcelona brothel (Avignon being the name of a street): three appear to be wearing African masks; two may have been modeled after his lover, Fernande Olivier. Appropriating forms from prehistoric Iberian sculpture, he no longer paints her in the sweet terms of his Rose Period (1904–06). These women unashamedly return the viewer's gaze as if challenging sexual, moral, or colonial judgment. Picasso was aware of rising public opinion against the Belgian genocide of the Congolese, as depicted in Joseph Conrad's novel *Heart of Darkness*. His bold willingness to adopt styles unfamiliar to Western audiences marks Picasso as one of the century's most radical avant garde artists.

3-SECOND THRASH
Picasso's *Les Demoiselles d'Avignon* was so shockingly Modern and proto-Cubist, that one of his avant-garde fellow artists, Georges Braque, likened its effect to drinking kerosene!

3-MINUTE THOUGHT
Picasso's African Period, 1907–09, which overlapped with Cubism, 1909–14, was dramatically influenced by African art. He sometimes denied any African inspiration, which is curious considering that one of his colleagues stole African art from the Trocadero Museum so that Picasso might study it at length. *Demoiselles* marks the beginning of quintessential Picasso characteristics that defined his art: dissonance, geometric shapes, and multiple perspectives.

RELATED TOPICS
See also
THE RITE OF SPRING
page 36

RED RUBBER SCANDAL IN THE BELGIAN CONGO
page 136

3-SECOND BIOGRAPHIES
PAUL CÉZANNE
1839–1906
French artist who inspired Modernism and Cubism

GEORGES BRAQUE
1882–1963
French artist who collaborated with Picasso to invent Cubism

DIEGO RIVERA
1886–1957
Mexican painter influenced by Modernism while living in Paris, who painted anticolonial murals on his return to Mexico

30-SECOND TEXT
Grace Chee

Stylized representations of the human face and figure in traditional African sculpture powerfully inspired Picasso.

THE RITE OF SPRING (*LE SACRE DU PRINTEMPS*)

the 30-second history

When the music opened the premiere of Igor Stravinsky's ballet *The Rite of Spring* on May 29, 1913 in Paris's brand-new Théâtre des Champs-Elysées, a whisper began among the audience. It grew louder as the Ballets Russes troupe took to the stage wearing folkloric costumes of Russian peasants, dazzling with color and geometric shapes, and quite unlike the diaphanous flowing gowns typically worn by ballet dancers. Then, the dancing started. There were no graceful leaps, floating hand movements, angelic postures. Instead, dancers pounded the ground with their leaps, shook their long braids and conical hats, and moved in syncopation against the rhythms of the music. The performance prompted a riot, the scandalized audience responding with jeers and catcalls so loud that the dancers could not hear the music. Choreographed by Vaslav Nijinsky, *The Rite of Spring* shocked the Parisian upper classes by telling the story of "Northern savages" in Pagan Russia celebrating the return of spring with dancing and fortune-telling. In the final act, a young maiden is sacrificed by dancing herself to death. Although its first audience hated it, *The Rite of Spring* is now hailed as a masterpiece of Modernism. In the century since its debut it has inspired countless musicians and artists, especially in jazz and modern dance.

3-SECOND THRASH
Stravinsky's *The Rite of Spring* brought the ballet world crashing down upon the French aristocracy with its modern rhythms and movements.

3-MINUTE THOUGHT
The subtitle of *The Rite of Spring* is "Pictures of Pagan Russia in Two Parts." When it debuted in 1913, the Russian Orthodox Church was deeply entwined with the governance of the Russian Empire. With the Bolshevik Revolution of 1917 and the subsequent creation of the Soviet Union in 1922, official religions were abolished. Instead, the communist government promoted gosateizm, or state atheism, and suppressed any expression of religious worship.

RELATED TOPICS
See also
GLOBAL BROADCAST OF "ALL YOU NEED IS LOVE"
page 26

LES DEMOISELLES D'AVIGNON
page 34

"THE PEANUT VENDOR"
page 42

3-SECOND BIOGRAPHIES
IGOR STRAVINSKY
1882–1971
Russian composer and conductor

VASLAV NIJINSKY
1890–1950
Russian ballet dancer and choreographer

30-SECOND TEXT
Sara Patenaude

Rites unleashed—Stravinsky and Nijinsky brought the vitality and energy of pagan folk culture into the refined setting of the Parisian ballet.

THE JAZZ SINGER

the 30-second history

The first feature-length studio motion picture with synchronized dialogue ("talkie"), this movie starred Al Jolson as a man caught between his Jewish faith and the prospects of a successful singing career. All six of Jolson's musical performances in the movie featured sound using a process called Vitaphone, the dialogue and music came from a phonograph connected to the film's projector. Jolson's dynamic performances left audiences mesmerized and sometimes nearly riotous. At the movie's premiere police were on hand to control the loud and boisterous crowd, who by the movie's end were nearly hysterical. *The Jazz Singer*'s broad success signaled the beginning of the end of the silent era and helped save a cash-strapped Warner Brothers Studios. The movie, directed by Alan Crosland, won a special Academy Award the first year they were presented (1929), though it was not allowed to compete against the silent films nominated for Outstanding Picture. The movie is based on the short story by Samuel Raphaelson entitled *The Day of Atonement* and was adapted into a play, which has also been made into two other feature films and for television. It helped define early Hollywood Jewish sensibilities and the conflict many had between their traditional, pious past and the modern age.

3-SECOND THRASH
The Jazz Singer brought sound to the big screen and complicated accepted racial boundaries, making it both timeless classic and subject of endless debate.

3-MINUTE THOUGHT
The lasting impact of *The Jazz Singer* went beyond the demise of the silent movie era. The film also brought African-American music to white audiences. Many African-Americans at the time of the movie's release embraced the struggle of Jolson's character. But its use of "blackface," a technique common to early 20th-century white performers whose performances all too often mocked rather than respected African-American culture, has remained a source of controversy.

RELATED TOPICS
See also
"THE PEANUT VENDOR"
page 42

"I HAVE A DREAM"
page 84

THE WALL STREET CRASH
page 102

3-SECOND BIOGRAPHIES
AL JOLSON
1886–1950
Jewish American singer and entertainer

ALAN CROSLAND
1894–1936
American stage actor then director of dozens of silent and sound features

SAMSON RAPHAELSON
1894–1983
American playwright and screenwriter

30-SECOND TEXT
Cary D. Harlow

With a lead actor of Jewish heritage performing in "blackface," The Jazz Singer examines American identities.

AL JOLSON in "THE JAZZ SINGER"

October 25, 1881
Born in Málaga, Spain

1897
Enters Spain's foremost art school, Madrid's Royal Academy of San Fernando, but quickly drops out

1900–04
Joins the avant garde in Paris. In 1901 his close friend Carles Casagemas commits suicide, beginning Picasso's Blue Period (1901–04)

1904–06
Falls in love with French artist-model Fernande Olivier, the start of Picasso's Rose Period (1904–06)

1907–09
Invents Cubism, with Georges Braque. Paints *Les Demoiselles d'Avignon* (1907–09 is Picasso's African Period, 1909–14 his Cubist Period)

1918
Marries Russian ballerina Olga Khokhlova

1925
Exhibits his Cubist art with the Surrealists

1927
Begins affair with French model, 17-year-old Marie-Thérèse Walter

1936–7
Paints *Guernica* (1937) and *Weeping Woman* (1937) with Croatian photographer-artist Dora Maar as his lover, muse, photographer, and collaborator

1943
Begins relationship with 21-year-old artist Françoise Gilot

1949
Picasso's *Dove* becomes international peace symbol

1953
Begins relationship with Jacqueline Roque; meets (Lydia) Sylvette David, who models for a series of portraits

1957
Miles Davis's album *Miles Ahead* includes "Blues for Pablo," as if in tribute to Picasso's contribution to the meaning of blue

1961
Marries Jacqueline Roque, who becomes the subject of numerous art pieces

1966
Museum of Modern Art in New York, in conjunction with the Louvre and the Tate Gallery, exhibits the first comprehensive overview of his sculptures

April 8, 1973
Dies in Mougins, France, at the age of 91

Pablo Picasso, whose prolific art

reflected the loves and events of his life, helped shape modern art and profoundly impacted on popular culture. While he and Braque invented Cubism, and influenced other modern styles, Picasso was fiercely independent, evading categories. Anchored by the women of his life, his art flowed through "periods," yet remained consistently modern, quintessentially Picasso.

Trained by his artist father, José Ruiz y Blasco, Picasso furthered his craft after he left Spain in 1900 to join the Paris *avant garde*. The suicide of a close friend informed his sad Blue Period. After Picasso first fell in love, with French artist-model Fernande Olivier, idyllic, dream-like scenes colored his Rose Period. Then, Picasso's art shifted, after studying Iberian and West African art. *Les Demoiselles d'Avignon* (1907), marked not only the prototype of his Cubist style, but the start of the characteristics that thereafter defined his art—dissonance, geometric shapes, and multiple perspectives— all rejecting traditional representations of reality. Marriage to Olga Khokhlova in 1918, at her insistence, induced a brief stint at neoclassicism. Shortly after, his art screeched at the constraints of high-society conventional married life. With his next relationship, with the scandalously young Marie-Thérèse Walter, his art shifted to express a voluptuous sensuality. This period intersected with the Surrealists, and inspired them, in emotional expressiveness, but not their psycho-automatism.

Picasso's art took on a new political and intellectually dramatic turn with Dora Maar, a Croatian photographer-artist who became his collaborator, lover, model, and muse. Maar pushed the previously self-proclaimed apolitical artist, especially after the Nazi-fascist bombing of Spanish town Gernika. She photographed Picasso painting *Guernica* (1937) in stages and modeled for a series evoking the traditional Spanish Virgin weeping glass tears, *The Weeping Woman* (1937). *Guernica* (*guerre*, French for war) exhibited around the world and, respecting Picasso's wishes, only returned to Spain after democracy was restored in 1981. His pacifist outcry is epitomized by *The Charnel House* (1945), *Dove* (1949), and *Massacre in Korea* (1951).

Even in the aftermath of such powerful pieces, Picasso remained prolific and financially successful, producing prints, paintings, ceramics, sculptures, and tapestries. A series of portraits, *Sylvette* (1955) features a platonic young friend whose disheveled ponytails became an iconic look for young women; Brigitte Bardot copied it and asked Picasso to paint her. Sylvette may also have inspired Picasso's 1967 statue, a gift to Chicago and known as the "Chicago Picasso." Picasso is known less for his sculptures, perhaps because he was reluctant to part with any. In his lifetime he produced some 50,000 pieces of art, including paintings, sculptures, ceramics, drawings, and tapestries, with a monumental impact on modern art.

Grace Chee

"THE PEANUT VENDOR"

the 30-second history

Once upon a time, where you lived determined the music you listened to, because all music was performed live by actual musicians. The advent of phonograph players and 78rpm records in the early 20th century radically transformed the music industry as well as local musical tastes and styles. By the 1930s, technological and commercial innovations allowed people around the globe to listen to exactly the same musical performance. The first song to be shared globally was probably "The Peanut Vendor," which sold well over 1 million copies in the early 1930s. Its global success was probably because Cuban rumba was itself a complex music created by the fusion of several different regional music styles. Rooted in rhythms and dance brought to the Caribbean by enslaved Africans, the melody was also informed by Spanish and North African phrasing and instruments. A dash of jazz (another global hybrid) via American influence in Cuba made for a sound that was at once familiar and exotic to global audiences. Musicians around the world were inspired not only to cover the song, but also to incorporate elements of rumba into their own compositions. The song remained a hit throughout much of the 20th century, being recorded over 150 times.

3-SECOND THRASH
The 1930 release of a recording of "The Peanut Vendor" initiated a global rumba craze and was likely the first "world music" hit.

3-MINUTE THOUGHT
In 1930, Don Azpiazú and his Havana Casino Orchestra recorded an already-popular Latin tune entitled "The Peanut Vendor" for Victor Records in New York City. Distributed on 78rpm records that were played on wind-up Victrola record players, the tune attracted fans in the US, the Caribbean, Latin America, and Europe. Traveling through networks of colonial trade, the song was a hit across much of Africa, in the Middle East, and even Asia.

RELATED TOPICS
See also
TRANSISTOR
page 22

GLOBAL BROADCAST OF "ALL YOU NEED IS LOVE"
page 26

THE WORLD WIDE WEB
page 28

THE JAZZ SINGER
page 38

BOLLYWOOD
page 48

3-SECOND BIOGRAPHIES
MOISÉS SIMONS
1889–1945
Cuban-born jazz pianist and composer

DON AZPIAZÚ
1893–1943
Cuban band leader

30-SECOND TEXT
Jonathan T. Reynolds

Heard all around the world, "The Peanut Vendor," written by Moisés Simons, was a global hit in the hands of Don Azpiazú.

PONG

the 30-second history

On-screen games were conceived back in the 1940s, using vacuum tubes to simulate a radar display. Following the invention of the transistor in 1947, various electronic games were produced in the ensuing decades, but they failed to gain popularity with the pinball-game bar crowd due to complex rules and operating systems. In 1972, the Atari Corporation was formed and Allan Alcorn, a new employee, was charged with creating a table tennis-like game for training purposes. PONG had two paddles that players moved vertically and a "ball" that picked up speed as the game progressed. A PONG prototype was installed in a local bar owned by a friend of Atari's founder. After two weeks, Alcorn was called to fix the game, which was experiencing operating problems; he found that the coin mechanism was jammed with quarters, prompting Atari to market PONG as a commercial arcade game. Home versions ensued in 1975, selling 150,000 units that Christmas, and several copycat versions were released thereafter. In 1977, Atari introduced the Atari 2600 Video Computer System. By the 1980s, a Video Computer System was a much-requested Christmas present, and video game arcades became the social hotspot for a generation of young people. Today, more than half of American households contain at least one current-generation gaming system.

RELATED TOPICS
See also
TRANSISTOR
page 22

THE WORLD WIDE WEB
page 28

3-SECOND BIOGRAPHIES
ALLAN ALCORN
1948–
American computer scientist and software engineer credited with creating PONG who later became an Apple Fellow and consultant to various technology companies

NOLAN BUSHNELL
1943–
American entrepreneur and founder of Atari, credited with Bushnell's Law, which states that an enjoyable video game should be "easy to learn and difficult to master"

30-SECOND TEXT
Laura J. Lee

Play it again ... the challenge of pioneering arcade game PONG hooked 1970s gamers and was also a hit with the home market.

3-SECOND THRASH
It's hard to believe, with the realistic graphics and complex storylines of video games today, that the gaming craze started with a simple line-and-dot game.

3-MINUTE THOUGHT
While PONG was the first commercially successful video game, it was not an original concept. The Magnavox Odyssey console, released in 1972, featured a game called Tennis, on which PONG was reportedly modeled. (Magnavox settled a case against Atari for patent infringement.) Atari set PONG apart from similar games through sound effects and altering the ball's return angle. More complex versions helped Atari achieve a leading position in the video-game industry.

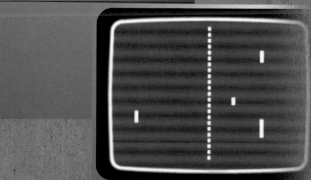

WOODSTOCK

the 30-second history

3-SECOND THRASH
Billed as "breakfast in bed
for 400,000" by Master of
Ceremonies Wavy Gravy,
Woodstock went on to
become an icon of Sixties
music and counterculture.

3-MINUTE THOUGHT
Woodstock seemed
destined for failure. Poor
planning, overcrowding,
delays, and heavy rain
combined to create an
apparent disaster. Yet, the
hippies, their ideals held
high, banded together for
peace and love. They
danced and smoked pot.
Some skinny-dipped to the
backdrop of antiwar cries
and the music of Arlo
Guthrie, Jimi Hendrix, and
others. It is difficult to
measure Woodstock's true
impact, but its legacy
echoes on in protestors,
freethinkers, and lovers
around the world today.

As the turbulent 1960s drew to
a close, America's hippie counterculture had
nearly washed away all of what it viewed as the
meaningless ideals of the baby-boomers for
its own set of utopian beliefs: world peace,
harmony, and free will. There had been
successful music festivals before, like the 1967
Monterey Pop festival, but nothing as ambitious
as the proposed event in a little town in the
Catskill Mountains. The Woodstock Festival, an
Aquarian Exposition, was set for August 15–17,
1969 and billed as "Three Days of Love and
Peace," which protested the United States'
ongoing involvement in the Vietnam War. The
festival was originally planned for Wallkill, New
York, but when the local government withheld
the required permits it was moved and approved
to be staged on Max Yasgur's Farm in Bethel.
With 200,000 people expected, and 185,000
tickets already sold, a rush to prepare the new
venue was too much for the little town to
handle. Traffic backed up, food and water was
inadequate, and to make matters worse, an
estimated 400,000–500,000 people arrived.
Nevertheless, the show went on. More than a
victory of cooperation over organization,
Woodstock came to define a generation.

RELATED TOPICS
See also
GLOBAL BROADCAST OF "ALL
YOU NEED IS LOVE"
page 26

"THE PEANUT VENDOR"
page 42

THE YEAR OF THE
BARRICADES
page 86

3-SECOND BIOGRAPHIES
JAMES MARSHALL "JIMI"
HENDRIX
1942–70
American rock guitarist

ARLO DAVY GUTHRIE
1947–
American folk musician

30-SECOND TEXT
Timothy D. Sofranko

*Over three days,
Friday–Sunday, 32
acts—including Joan
Baez, Grateful Dead,
Santana, Jefferson
Airplane, and The
Who—entertained the
peace-loving crowd.*

BOLLYWOOD

the 30-second history

Even if you've never seen one of its movies, the word Bollywood will likely conjure an image of bright colors, music, and people singing and dancing, imbuing the invigorating rhythm with everything they cannot say or show about three little letters that are so closely censored: sex. "Bollywood" generally refers to movies made in Bombay (Mumbai). Though India has many languages, these movies are in Hindi, the common trade language, and have become part of a national identity, a unifying agent for a country with a huge and diverse population. Bollywood movies may be in any number of genres, though song and dance will be integral to the plot. In 1913 India's first full-length, *Raja Harishchandra*, was released. Less than 20 years on, *Alam Ara*, India's first movie with talking and singing, debuted in Bombay in 1931. The 1950s and 60s are often termed Indian cinema's Golden Age, producing a number of memorable movies. In the 1970s, the Masala movie became popular. As the name suggests, it is a spicy combination of genres for maximum entertainment and escapist impact. In that decade the term "Bollywood" was coined after India first exceeded the US output of movies being produced. In fact, the Indian Film Industry holds the Guinness record for the largest annual movie output—800–1,000 movies: double Hollywood's number!

RELATED TOPIC
See also
THE JAZZ SINGER
page 38

3-SECOND BIOGRAPHIES
MANMOHAN DESAI
1937–94
Indian director and producer; considered the father of the Masala movie

AMIT KHANNA
1951–
Indian journalist, producer, writer, lyricist; credited with coining the term Bollywood

30-SECOND TEXT
Kristin Hornsby

3-SECOND THRASH
Selling more tickets than Hollywood movies, Bollywood productions are show-stopping feasts for the senses.

3-MINUTE THOUGHT
Bollywood movies tend to be melodramatic, and the romantic leads may not even kiss when they finally get together! Why? The Central Board of Film Certification oversees all movie that are released in India to ensure they fit a certain standard. Nudity, smoking (a recent rule), religious or ethnic violence, French kissing ... anything the board finds offensive must be left on the cutting-room floor.

In Bollywood love and longing find colorful expression in often highly choreographed but never explicit blockbusters.

WAR & CONFLICTS

Aryan state A core component of the German Nazi Party's political ideology was that German greatness stemmed from the fact that Aryans represented a superior human race, and that Germans were the purest of all Aryan peoples. Such ideas of racial superiority were a core element of fascism.

Beer Hall Putsch Inspired by Italian fascist Benito Mussolini's successful takeover in Italy in 1922, in November 1923 roughly 2,000 German Nazi Party supporters, led by Adolf Hitler, attempted to overthrow the Weimar government of Germany. The coup failed and led to Hitler's conviction and imprisonment, but it also brought him considerable fame among German extremists.

Cold War This term describes the competition between the United States and the Soviet Union from after the Second World War (1939–45) to the collapse of the Soviet Union in 1989–91. The term "Cold War" highlighted that the conflict was more about ideas and political allegiance among allies than about warfare. The Cold War was nonetheless very hot in places such as Korea, Angola, and Afghanistan.

The Manhattan Project In 1939, the United States launched a top-secret research program to investigate the potential of atomic weapons. By 1942, in cooperation with the British and Canadians, the project was well under way: by 1945 it had succeeded in producing the Trinity test bomb and the weapons used against Nagasaki and Hiroshima. In doing so the project launched the Atomic Age and set the stage for the Cold War.

Mujahideen This is an Arabic term that translates loosely as "holy warrior"— designating someone who fights against the enemies of Islam. The term gained wide recognition during the Soviet occupation of Afghanistan in the 1980s, when the US government funded, armed, and advised the anti-Soviet Mujahideen, who eventually drove out the Soviet forces.

Social Darwinism This concept, which argues that superior societies "naturally" subjugate inferior ones, first gained currency in the late 19th century to justify European colonialism. In the 20th century, however, it was increasingly used to justify anti-Semitism, racism, eugenics, and genocide—not only in fascist states, but also in some democracies.

Treaty of Versailles The Treaty of Versailles of 1919 between the Allied Powers and Germany is one of the most controversial topics of the 20th century. The demands that Germany accept guilt for the First World War (1914–18), pay substantial reparations, cede lands, and demilitarize are all considered factors that helped facilitate the rise of German fascism and set the world on the path to the Second World War (1939–45).

Third Reich The period from the rise of the German Nazi Party in 1933 to the surrender of Germany in 1945 is often dubbed the "Third Reich," meaning "third nation" or "third empire." The term was chosen to invoke the idea that the German people had returned to greatness under the Nazis.

Viêt Minh The Independence Party of Vietnam, the Viêt Minh, was formed in 1941 to oppose French colonialism. During the Second World War (1939–45), they fought against the Japanese and their Vichy French Allies. With Soviet support, over the next four decades they would fight against the French, US, and Chinese in pursuit of Vietnamese independence.

THE BOXER REBELLION

the 30-second history

Between 1839 and 1895 China lost three wars and considerable autonomy to Western powers and Japan. In 1898 the young Manchu emperor, advised by reformers, called for dramatic modernization. But Empress-Dowager Cixi and her conservative allies blocked the proposals, arrested the reformers, put the emperor under house arrest, promoted an antiforeign atmosphere, and encouraged the Chinese to organize militias. Many Chinese resented the impact of Western-financed modernization, especially railways, on their lives. Floods, famine, and drought affected parts of northern China. The ensuing tensions sparked the Boxer Rebellion in 1900 to drive foreigners out of China. The Boxers, a peasant, anti-Western, anti-Christian secret society, attacked foreigners and Chinese Christians in northern China, occupied Beijing, and besieged foreign embassies, while the Qing declared war on foreign powers. But British, American, and French forces routed the Boxers and occupied Beijing, while the Qing was made to pay another huge indemnity to Western powers and permit foreign military forces in China. Europeans talked openly of dismantling China; Russians used the rebellion to occupy Manchuria. The rebellion's failure left China in an even weaker position than before and primed for more far-reaching revolution.

RELATED TOPIC
See also
THE LONG MARCH
page 76

3-SECOND BIOGRAPHIES
EMPRESS DOWAGER CIXI
1835–1908
Powerful Manchu imperial concubine who unofficially led China's Qing dynasty (1875–1908)

KANG YOUWEI
1858–1927
A major Chinese reformer whose advice to the emperor sparked the 100 Days of Reform that helped inspire the reactionary Boxer Rebellion in response

30-SECOND TEXT
Craig Lockard

3-SECOND THRASH
The Boxer Rebellion was a violent uprising in response to Western pressure on China, but government-supported attacks on foreigners led to humiliating defeat.

3-MINUTE THOUGHT
Defeat of the Boxers led to frantic efforts at modernization. Fearing China might soon be divided into colonies, the Qing rulers raised military spending, strengthened provincial governments, abolished the 2,000-year-old Confucian examination system, sent 10,000 pupils to Japan, and set up Western-style schools that enrolled only a fraction of China's school-age children. The reforms were often slow and ineffective. In 1911–12 a more radical revolution swept away the Qing dynasty and established a republic.

The "Society of Righteous and Harmonious Fists," known as the Boxers, were local farmers and peasants whose livelihoods had been lost through imperialism and a series of natural disasters.

JAPANESE DEFEAT OF RUSSIA

the 30-second history

RELATED TOPICS
See also
THE BOXER REBELLION
page 54

THE BATTLE OF THE SOMME
page 58

3-SECOND BIOGRAPHIES
TŌGŌ HEIHACHIHŌ
1848–1934
Admiral in the Japanese
Imperial Navy

WILGELM VITGEFT
1847–1904
Admiral in the Imperial
Russian Navy

STEPAN OSIPOVICH MAKAROV
1849–1904
Vice Admiral in the Imperial
Russian Navy

3-SECOND THRASH
In 1904 and 1905, Japan stunned the world by defeating Imperial Russia in a series of land and naval engagements.

3-MINUTE THOUGHT
At the beginning of the 20th century, Russian desires for a warm-water port on the Pacific and Japanese aspirations for control over Korean and Manchurian resources exploded into warfare. Western observers expected the Russian juggernaut easily to defeat the upstart Japanese state. Japan's decisive land victories and near-total destruction of the Russian navy upset both the global balance of power and Western assumptions about racial superiority.

After being shocked out of isolation by American gunboat diplomacy in 1853, Japan began a breakneck pursuit of political and industrial modernization. Crucial to the process was the building of a modern army and navy. This undertaking required access to resources and markets not available within its borders. Like the Western powers, Japan looked to imperial conquest to help fuel and fund its expansion, setting its new military sights on Korea and northern China. Meantime, Russia was seeking to anchor its expansion eastward. Port Arthur, a warm-water port on the Yellow Sea that could be accessed via the recently completed trans-Siberian railway, proved exactly the location the Russians sought, setting Russia and Japan on a collision course. After diplomatic efforts failed, Japan launched a combined land and sea attack in February 1904, sinking and damaging several Russian ships. By August it had destroyed much of Russia's Pacific fleet and seized Port Arthur. Russia responded by sending its Baltic fleet to the Pacific. Despite significantly outnumbering their Japanese adversaries, the new Russian fleet was nearly annihilated in the decisive Battle of Tsushima on May 27–29, 1905. The Russo-Japanese war represented the first "modern" naval conflict and paved the way for the Japanese annexation of Korea and invasion of China.

30-SECOND TEXT
Jonathan Reynolds

The Japanese navy's defeat of its Russian counterpart in May 1905 occurred in the Tsushima Strait between Korea and Japan—and sent shock waves around the world.

THE BATTLE OF THE SOMME

the 30-second history

The **bloodiest battle in the** history of mankind was waged from July 1 to November 13, 1916, as the British and French fought tooth and nail to recover territory in France from the invading Germans. While it was two years into the First World War (1914–18), "the Somme" marked the loss of a generation's innocence as eyes were opened to the terrible nature of modern warfare. Men on both sides died, not through lack of professionalism or spirit on their part, but because the world's military leadership still underestimated the strength of dug-in positions and the dangers of assaulting them. In the first afternoon, the British sustained more than 55,000 casualties. Brave men charged into razor wire and the teeth of machine guns by the thousand; one division, the Eighth from III Corps, suffered 80 percent casualties in the battle's first ten minutes. The Allies endured, regrouped, stood fast against German counterattacks, and tried again, and again, and again. Forward progress came slowly but steadily, and when November's cold halted the campaign, both sides breathed sighs of relief and let the battle die with the Allied trenches having advanced roughly 5 miles (8km).

RELATED TOPICS
See also
JAPANESE DEFEAT OF RUSSIA
page 56

THE FIRST ARAB-ISRAELI WAR
page 64

DIEN BIEN PHU
page 66

SOVIET DEFEAT IN AFGHANISTAN
page 68

3-SECOND BIOGRAPHIES
DOUGLAS HAIG
1861–1928
Field Marshal and leader of the British Army during the Somme

ROBERT GRAVES
1895–1985
British novelist, soldier, and poet, injured at the Somme

30-SECOND TEXT
Russell Zimmerman

Scarlet corn poppies, which grew after the war on fields ravaged by conflict, became a potent symbol of the youthful lives lost in battle.

3-SECOND THRASH
The Battle of the Somme raged for four-and-a-half months, resulting in more than 1 million casualties, so that roughly 15 miles (25km) of trench could advance 5 miles (8km).

3-MINUTE THOUGHT
Attitudes toward the First World War changed when it became clear how wasteful inflexible strategies were when they clashed with industrialized firepower. The British army was largely composed of the "pal battalions," young volunteers who had joined up in groups from neighborhood clubs and soccer or rugby teams. When word, and even documentary footage, of the Somme's butchery reached the Home Front, a nation was left asking high command and their government one terrible question about their sons' deaths: "Why?"

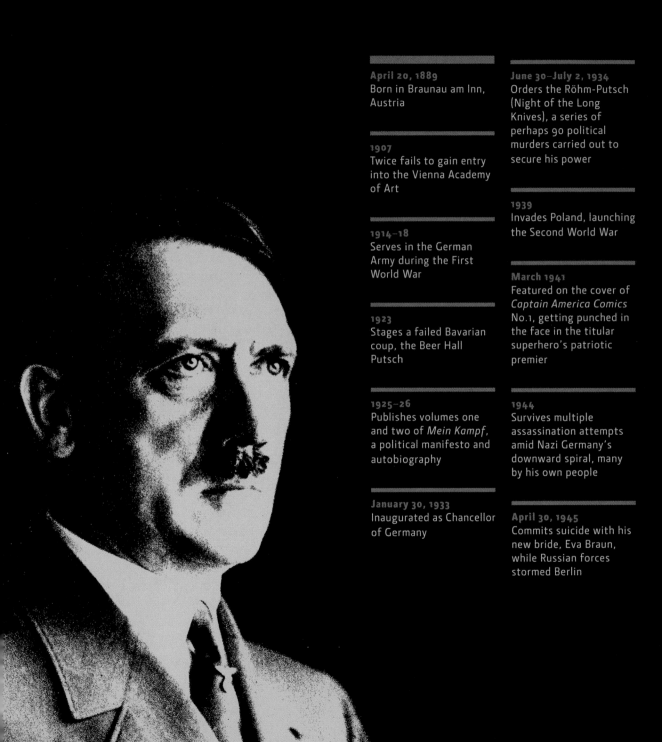

April 20, 1889
Born in Braunau am Inn, Austria

1907
Twice fails to gain entry into the Vienna Academy of Art

1914–18
Serves in the German Army during the First World War

1923
Stages a failed Bavarian coup, the Beer Hall Putsch

1925–26
Publishes volumes one and two of *Mein Kampf*, a political manifesto and autobiography

January 30, 1933
Inaugurated as Chancellor of Germany

June 30–July 2, 1934
Orders the Röhm-Putsch (Night of the Long Knives), a series of perhaps 90 political murders carried out to secure his power

1939
Invades Poland, launching the Second World War

March 1941
Featured on the cover of *Captain America Comics* No.1, getting punched in the face in the titular superhero's patriotic premier

1944
Survives multiple assassination attempts amid Nazi Germany's downward spiral, many by his own people

April 30, 1945
Commits suicide with his new bride, Eva Braun, while Russian forces stormed Berlin

ADOLF HITLER

The name Adolf Hitler has become synonymous with evil, racism, and totalitarian dictatorship; to much of the world, Hitler has become a symbol of oppression and failure, but to modern neo-Nazis and others who still follow his ideology, he is seen as something of a martyred patron.

Hitler's early years were marked by poverty and a growing public hatred of liberals, Jews, and Marxists. He was also privately disdainful of and bitter toward Christianity, the Catholic church in particular, for most of his adult life.

A frustrated veteran of the First World War, Hitler ranted against Germany's leadership to gain popular support, blaming the nation's economic woes on the external pressures of the Treaty of Versailles and on internal betrayals by imagined Jewish conspiracies. His National Socialist German Worker's Party—the Nazis—built a political platform on shared hatred and bitterness, growing stronger until Hitler became the most powerful man in Germany (partially through the violent oppression of his rivals). The Third Reich was born, and he dreamed of an empire that would last a thousand years.

The German state under Hitler was uniquely celebrative of the "German" spirit, while simultaneously oppressive of outside influences or those who disagreed with precisely what being a good German meant. A fine example of this is the Nazi Party's schizophrenic celebration/ suppression of music and other art, with loyal party members being allowed to flourish, and talented artists who disagreed with the Nazis being harshly censored or punished. Hitler and Propaganda Minister Joseph Goebbels adored Beethoven and Wagner as masters of good German music, and even found some common ground with them regarding Beethoven's Teutonic pride, and Wagner's anti-Semitism.

Hitler took a fierce pride in the German– Aryan—state that flourished under him, and soon ordered the recovery of ground lost in the First World War and, in fact, the taking of new territory entirely. Hitler's aggressive expansion soon prompted the outbreak of the Second World War. The Nazis swiftly occupied most of Western Europe, spreading their doctrine at bayonet-point and grinding dissention beneath the treads of their tanks. Free to act upon the promises and hatreds that had brought him to power, Hitler oversaw the deaths of millions in the infamous concentration camps.

While the Second World War initially went well for Hitler and his allies, another of his decisions, Operation Barbarossa—the betrayal and invasion of the Soviet Union—marked the war's turning point. Fighting on two fronts, Nazi Germany began to crumble. Hitler's madness led to increasingly erratic and irrational decisions until the Reich fell. In a bunker beneath Berlin, Hitler escaped capture by ending his own life.

Russell Zimmerman

HIROSHIMA

the 30-second history

The watershed moment of the first atomic bomb—8:15am on August 6, 1945—came to symbolize not only the beginning of the end of the Second World War, but also the opening of a nuclear Pandora's box. This sparked the start of an arms race that showed man to be his own greatest enemy. US President Truman gave the order to unleash atomic destruction upon Japan after the country refused to respond to the Potsdam Conference's ultimatum of surrender. As a military and industrial target, Hiroshima was intentionally spared conventional bombing so that the results of the atomic weapon could be accurately measured in the aftermath. Developed through the $2 billion Manhattan Project, the first bomb, named "Little Boy," exploded with the radiation and heat energy equivalent to 16 kilotons of TNT. The bomb was dropped from the *Enola Gay*, a B-29 Superfortress aircraft. Hiroshima was decimated in literally a flash; a 10,830°F (6,000°C) fireball and shockwave of pressure obliterated everything within a radius of 1 mile (1.6km). Damage from the blast encompassed a 4.4-mile (7-km) area from the epicenter of the blast and people continued to die from the effects of radiation poisoning, days, weeks, months, and even years later.

3-SECOND THRASH
The first use of a nuclear weapon helped end the Second World War, but launched an era of potential nuclear conflict and the Cold War.

3-MINUTE THOUGHT
The challenge of Hiroshima's recovery was twofold. The bomb was so devastating that both physical and human resources were vaporized, leaving victims with nowhere to turn for help; 90 percent of the medical professionals were dead or disabled. Wilfred Burchett, the first Western journalist to have documented the effects of the "atomic plague," was quickly censored from publishing his reports. As a result medical personnel were not able to treat victims adequately.

RELATED TOPICS
See also
SPLITTING THE ATOM
page 16

ALBERT EINSTEIN
page 20

3-SECOND BIOGRAPHIES
JULIUS ROBERT OPPENHEIMER
1904–67
American physicist, most famously known as the "father of the atomic bomb" for his leadership on the Manhattan Project

WILFRED BURCHETT
1911–83
Australian journalist, the first foreign correspondent to enter Hiroshima and report on the devastating effects

PAUL TIBBETS
1915–2007
US pilot whose plane, named after his mother, dropped the first atomic bomb on Hiroshima

30-SECOND TEXT
Rita R. Thomas

The US bombings of Japan are the only two uses of nuclear weapons in war.

THE FIRST ARAB–ISRAELI WAR

the 30-second history

The 1948 war was a complicated result of European colonialism and racism and new national aspirations. Jewish settlement in Palestine was driven by well-established fears of anti-Semitism in Europe. During the Second World War, extremist Jewish groups in the region used bombings and attacks to try to force the British to allow more Jewish emigration. The postwar flood of Jewish refugees from Europe and elsewhere heightened Jewish–Palestinian tensions, with both populations committing atrocities. The newly established United Nations proposed the creation of two states with economic union. Most Palestinians rejected the plan because the proposed Palestinian borders were fragmented and separated by a single Israeli territory. Local conflicts grew into civil war, which burgeoned as newly independent Arab nations joined the conflict. The heavily outnumbered Israeli army was supplied with weapons and supplies by communist Czechoslovakia, allowing them to fight poorly coordinated Arab forces to a stalemate. When Egypt and other Arab states aligned with the Soviets in the 1950s, the United States began to support Israel. Arab–Israeli conflicts in 1967 and 1973 were flashpoints of Cold War tensions, and the plight of Palestinian refugees would become a focus for global Muslim discontent.

3-SECOND THRASH
A minor 20th-century war in terms of casualties, the 1948 Arab–Israeli War was among the most politically complex and influential conflicts of the century.

3-MINUTE THOUGHT
Colonized by the British in 1917, the region of Palestine became a destination for those seeking to create a Jewish state. This desire collided with the aspirations of local Palestinian and regional Arab populations to create independent states of their own following the Second World War. A UN partition plan proposed politically independent but economically interdependent states, but the partition collapsed in the face of local conflict that grew to include the newly independent Arab states.

RELATED TOPICS
See also
THE BOXER REBELLION
page 54

DIEN BIEN PHU
page 66

THE BANDUNG CONFERENCE
page 78

THE HOLOCAUST
page 140

3-SECOND BIOGRAPHIES
MENACHEM BEGIN
1913–92
Israeli militant and politician

YASSER ARAFAT
1929–2004
Palestinian militant and politician

30-SECOND TEXT
Jonathan T. Reynolds

The war made refugees of populations on both sides of the Israeli–Palestinian dispute and had repercussions that lasted for decades.

DIEN BIEN PHU

the 30-second history

During the First Indochina War
(1946–54) the French attempted to maintain
their colonial grip over Vietnam against the
communist-led Viêt Minh but got bogged down
in a "quicksand war." To regain the initiative, in
early 1954 they stationed large forces in a
remote valley along the border with Laos in
hopes of weakening Viêt Minh operations.
But they underestimated Viêt Minh capabilities
and commander Võ Nguyên Giáp's formidable
logistical preparations, which built roads into
Dien Bien Phu to transport troops, food, and
weapons, particularly artillery. By March
80,000 Viêt Minh troops surrounded the French
garrison and its 15,000 defenders. Three months
of fierce fighting, including artillery disabling the
airstrip for relief flights, devastated the garrison,
leaving only 3,000 healthy defenders. In early
May the Viêt Minh overran the base. The
fighting had left some 3,000 French dead and
5,000 wounded; the Viêt Minh lost 8,000 and
15,000 were wounded. The Viêt Minh force-
marched 6,000–8,000 French prisoners 500
miles (800km) to prison camps; only 10 percent
survived. The humiliating defeat stunned the
French public and caused the government to
collapse. The French abandoned their efforts,
negotiated a peace agreement at a conference
in Geneva in 1954, and went home.

3-SECOND THRASH
The Battle of Dien Bien
Phu in 1954, in which
communist forces
overwhelmed a key
French garrison, ultimately
brought an end to French
colonialism in Vietnam.

3-MINUTE THOUGHT
This battle dramatically
changed history. The
resulting Geneva
agreements divided
Vietnam into two
countries: communist-
ruled North and pro-
Western South. Cold War
tensions and nationalism
ensured further conflict.
The United States, which
had given massive aid to
the French against the
Viêt Minh, now assumed a
more prominent role in
Vietnam's affairs, resulting
in the Vietnam War. By
1975 US forces were gone
and Vietnam was reunited
under communist control.

RELATED TOPIC
See also
THE BOXER REBELLION
page 54

3-SECOND BIOGRAPHIES
GENERAL VÕ NGUYÊN GIÁP
1911–2013
Vietnamese general who led
communist resistance against
the Japanese in the Second
World War and French forces
in the First Indochina War

HO CHI MINH
1890–1969
Most important builder of
Vietnamese communism and
leader of North Vietnam
(1945–69)

30-SECOND TEXT
Craig Lockard

*Colonial rule began to
seem unsustainable
when, in a battle with
major historical
implications, a
Western army was
humiliated by a
formidable colonial
independence force in
March–May 1954.*

SOVIET DEFEAT IN AFGHANISTAN

the 30-second history

Afghanistan spent the late 1970s begging the Soviet Union for aid in a bitter sectarian conflict. While the civil war provided the USSR with its pretence for action, in many ways the ensuing invasion had imperialist underpinnings: to spread the Soviet bloc into the area, impress Middle Eastern nations, and gather natural resources. Rather than pacifying the country, the heavy Soviet military presence encouraged the rebellion, now united against a common foe to spread. Soon, the fundamentally atheist Soviets found themselves opposed by Muslim freedom fighters who were receiving support from the Soviets' secular Cold War rivals (these Mujahideen insurgents were commonly trained by Western CIA, MI6, and SAS advisors, for instance). Though often lacking in organization, the Mujahideen used sabotage, assassination, and other guerrilla tactics to resist their occupiers, and war dragged on, involving hundreds of thousands of casualties. The momentum of the conflict began to shift in the mid-1980s when the United States provided ground-to-air Stinger missiles, taking away the Soviet advantage of air superiority. The Soviets spent the latter half of the decade shifting the burden of maintaining security back to the Afghani army, prior to withdrawing completely.

RELATED TOPICS
See also
DIEN BIEN PHU
page 66

THE CUBAN MISSILE CRISIS
page 82

ARGENTINA'S DIRTY WAR
page 90

3-SECOND BIOGRAPHIES
HAZIFULLAH AMIN
1929–79
Afghan prime minister who urged early Muslim agitation

CHARLES WILSON
1933–2010
American politician responsible for "Operation Cyclone," the CIA operation that supplied military equipment to the Mujahideen

AHMAD SHAH MASSOUD
1953–2001
Afghan politician and freedom fighter during the Soviet occupation

30-SECOND TEXT
Russell Zimmerman

US military hardware combined with Mujahideen passion brought down the USSR.

3-SECOND THRASH
The Soviet Union invaded Afghanistan in 1979, but remained bogged down in guerrilla war for nearly a decade before a humiliating withdrawal.

3-MINUTE THOUGHT
The Soviets' invasion of Afghanistan has been called "Russia's Vietnam." In both cases, the guerrilla resistance was able to recruit based on powerful ideological differences, to blend with the civilian populace and often to leverage the brutality of the invaders against them by turning that, too, into a recruitment tool. Many of the Soviet disadvantages would come back to haunt a new wave of soldiers decades later, with NATO military operations in Afghanistan encountering the same frustrations.

POLITICS & SOCIETY

African National Congress (ANC) Initially formed in 1911, the African National Congress developed as the main opposition group to South African racial oppression. The party maintained a program of nonviolent resistance until the 1960s, at which point it accepted the necessity of violence to overturn South Africa's government. Following the collapse of apartheid in 1994, the ANC became the dominant political party in the country.

Bantustans After the creation of apartheid in 1948, the Native Reserves that comprised some 13 percent of the country were renamed Bantustans, which the South African government sought to identify as independent nations: this was a means of declaring nonwhites to be noncitizens of the country.

Cold War This term describes the competition between the United States and the Soviet Union from after the Second World War (1939–45) to the collapse of the Soviet Union in 1989–91. The term "Cold War" highlighted that the conflict was more about ideas and political allegiance among allies than about warfare. The Cold War was nonetheless very hot in places such as Korea, Angola, and Afghanistan.

ExComm The Executive Committee of the National Security Council (ExComm) was established in 1962 to provide a group of expert advisers to President John F. Kennedy during the Cuban Missile Crisis.

Nation Defined as a political system embodying the will and destiny of culturally homogeneous and geographically bounded population, the idea of the nation became the accepted norm for political organization in the 19th and 20th centuries. Unfortunately, few if any human populations are culturally homogeneous or geographically bounded.

National American Woman Suffrage Association Founded in 1890, this organization was established to advocate for Women's suffrage in the United States. Along with the somewhat more radical National Women's Party, the NAWSA campaigned successfully for the passage in 1920 of the 19th Amendment to the US constitution, which guaranteed women's right to vote. The groups would then unsuccessfully pursue the passage of the Equal Rights Amendment.

Non-Aligned Movement Founded in Belgrade in 1961, and building upon the 1955 Bandung Conference, the movement sought to establish a power block of nonaligned states as a counterweight to the Western and Eastern camps created by the Cold War. The countries of India, Yugoslavia, Ghana, Indonesia, and Egypt were particularly influential in setting the group's agenda.

Operation Condor Launched in 1975, this operation was a coordinated plan among Latin American military governments to eradicate left-wing intellectuals and activists from the region. With the knowledge and material aid of the United States, these states pursued programs of torture and assassination that resulted in the deaths of tens of thousands of individuals.

Prague Spring This term refers to a brief period of political liberalization that took place in Czechoslovakia in early 1968. Reforms included lifting restriction on travel, free speech, and religious worship. After brief negotiations, Warsaw Pact forces invaded Czechoslovakia in August and reversed the reforms.

Townships Under apartheid in South Africa, nonwhites were not allowed to live in cities. In order to meet the demand for labor in the cities townships were established outside urban areas where nonwhites were allowed to remain so long as they were employed in white areas.

"KAISER WILSON"

the 30-second history

The 19th Amendment, which guarantees American women the right to vote, was first introduced to Congress in 1878. Forty years later, women remained disenfranchised. Seeing an opportunity to further their cause, the National American Woman Suffrage Association made the controversial decision to support President Wilson in taking the USA into the First World War in 1917. Their strategy highlighted the hypocrisy of fighting for democracy in Europe while denying it to women at home. Suffragettes staged demonstrations against Wilson, with members of the more radical National Woman's Party (NWP) gaining a reputation for being particularly outspoken and using biting satire. A famous photograph shows a woman outside the White House holding a poster calling on "Kaiser Wilson" to support women's suffrage—a clear dig at the president who, for women, was no more an advocate of democracy than was Germany's Kaiser. The strategy worked. In his 1918 State of the Union Address Wilson officially announced his support for the amendment, which Congress passed in 1919. Use of wartime propaganda about democracy as leverage to demand the extension of sovereignty in the United States and elsewhere became a theme of the century, with similar tactics used by African-Americans and those under the yoke of colonial rule.

RELATED TOPICS
See also
THE BATTLE OF THE SOMME
page 58

THE PILL
page 124

3-SECOND BIOGRAPHIES
ELIZABETH CADY STANTON
& SUSAN B. ANTHONY
1815–1902 & 1820–1906
American social activists and coauthors of the 19th Amendment

CARRIE CHAPMAN CATT
1859–1947
American campaigner for women's suffrage and President of the National American Woman Suffrage Association

ALICE STOKES PAUL
1885–1977
American suffragette and leader of the NWP

30-SECOND TEXT
Sara Patenaude

Alice Paul (right) and others maneuvered President Wilson into support for women's suffrage.

3-SECOND THRASH
During the First World War, suffragettes used President Wilson's apparent hypocrisy over democracy as leverage to demand the right to vote for American women.

3-MINUTE THOUGHT
Suffragette vigils outside the White House provoked often hostile reaction; some of the so-called "silent sentinels" faced arrest. Nonetheless, their tactics and rhetoric drew attention to the issue of women's rights. Following the 19th Amendment success, the NWP supported the Equal Rights Amendment, which sought to guarantee equal rights for women. Though passed by Congress, it failed to gain enough state support for ratification and has never become law.

THE LONG MARCH
the 30-second history

The Long March changed the course of modern Chinese history, saving the growing communist movement from extinction in a civil war. Faced with the expansion of a revolutionary communist base in remote mountains in Jiangxi province (led by Mao Zedong) China's conservative, US-backed president, Chiang Kai-shek, had his army blockade the base to keep out essential supplies, forcing Mao to seek a safer base. In 1934 Mao's 100,000 soldiers and followers broke through the blockade and began the Long March, an epic journey. Mao's Red Army fought their way 6,000 miles (10,000km) on foot and horseback through 11 provinces, crossed 18 mountain ranges, forded 24 rivers, and slogged through swamps, losing 90 percent of their people to death or desertion. In late 1935 the ragtag survivors arrived in a poor northwestern province, moving into cave-like homes in hills around Yen'an city. The Long March saved the communists from elimination, making Mao the unchallenged Communist Party leader. But, still vulnerable to Chiang's larger, better-equipped forces, they would be saved by Japan's invasion of China in 1937, which forced Chiang to shift his military priorities to fighting the Japanese, allowing the communists to regroup and spread their message in wartime China.

RELATED TOPICS
See also
THE BOXER REBELLION
page 54

DIEN BIEN PHU
page 66

THE CULTURAL REVOLUTION
page 142

3-SECOND THRASH
During this epic journey in 1934–35, Mao Zedong's Communist Red Army fought their way 6,000 miles (10,000km) to establish a safe base for continuing their revolution.

3-MINUTE THOUGHT
Revolutions transformed various 20th-century societies, notably China and Russia. The instability following the collapse of imperial China led to chaos and a struggle between conservative, pro-Western nationalists and communist-led left-wing forces for control of China. The Long March and the Japanese invasion ultimately gave the communists the advantage and control of China, making Mao and the Chinese communists models for radicals elsewhere and upending the world's power balance.

3-SECOND BIOGRAPHIES
MAO ZEDONG
1893–1976
Leader of Chinese Communist Party and first chairman of the People's Republic of China between 1949 and 1976

CHIANG KAI-SHEK
1887–1975
Nationalist military leader who led the Republic of China, first in China and then Taiwan, from 1928 to 1975

30-SECOND TEXT
Craig Lockard

Mao's leadership sustained the Chinese communists through months of severe hardship. They became an inspiration to radicals the world over.

THE BANDUNG CONFERENCE

the 30-second history

3-SECOND THRASH
The Bandung Conference
of April 18–24, 1955
brought together Asian,
African, and Middle-
Eastern nations in their
fight for decolonization,
human rights, and
economic development.

3-MINUTE THOUGHT
The Non-Aligned
Movement put the United
States in a difficult political
situation. Under Franklin
D. Roosevelt the US had
condemned colonialism,
and had little choice but
to support continued
decolonization. And
yet, the US still needed
the former colonial
powers as Cold War allies.
As a result, the US was
forced constantly to
balance its stated political
ideals against harsh Cold
War realities.

The Bandung or Asian-African
Conference, took place in Bandung, Indonesia,
in April 1955. Representatives from 29 nations,
many of which had recently gained independence
from colonial rule, met to discuss the effects of
the growing Cold War between the United States
and the Soviet Union. India's Jawaharlal Nehru
was a vocal advocate of the movement. The
attending nations sought to create a nonaligned
"Third World" that would side with neither the US
nor the USSR in their fight over capitalism versus
communism. Instead, they sought solidarity with
one another, feeling that their concerns were not
being supported by either superpower. Delegates
called for an end to the twin forces of colonialism
and racism that still affected many African, Asian,
and Middle Eastern nations. They also sought
ways to increase economic development in their
countries. At the end of the conference the
representatives passed the ten-point "Declaration
on Promotion of World Peace and Cooperation,"
modeled on the United Nations Charter of
June 26, 1945, which called for international
respect for human rights, an end to racism,
and foreign policy that supported national
sovereignty and decolonization.

RELATED TOPICS
See also
SPUTNIK
page 24

THE LONG MARCH
page 76

THE CUBAN MISSILE CRISIS
page 82

THE CULTURAL REVOLUTION
page 142

3-SECOND BIOGRAPHIES
JAWAHARLAL NEHRU
1889–1964
First Prime Minister of India
(1947–64) following
independence from Britain

SUKARNO (SOEKARNO)
1901–70
First President of Indonesia
(1945–67) following
independence from the
Netherlands

30-SECOND TEXT
Sara Patenaude

*More than half the
world's population
was represented by
the 29 country
delegations at the
conference.*

AFGHANISTAN
BURMA
CAMBODJA
CEYLON
CHINA
EGYPT
ETHIOPIA
INDIA
IRAN
IRAQ
JAPAN
JORDAN
IAOS
LEBANON
LIBFRIA
LIBYA
NFPAI
PAKISTAN
PHILIPPINFS
SUDAN
SYRIA
THAILAND
TURKFY
VIETNAM

May 7, 1919
Born in Los Toldos, a village outside of the city of Junín, in the province of Buenos Aires, Argentina. Youngest of five children born to Juana Ibarguren and married rancher Juan Duarte

1934
Moves to Buenos Aires to pursue a career in the growing entertainment industry. Works as model, plays minor roles in theater and movie productions, acts in radio dramas

January 22, 1944
Meets General Juan Domingo Perón at a gala to benefit earthquake victims

October 18, 1945
Marries Juan Domingo Perón in a civil ceremony in Junín

December 9, 1945
Couple marries in a religious ceremony

June 4, 1946
Becomes First Lady when her husband is elected as president for the first of three terms

1947
As First Lady, Eva tours Europe, meeting numerous dignitaries and heads of state, such as Francisco Franco, Pope Pius XII, and Charles de Gaulle. Britain's King George VI refuses to receive her visit

July 8, 1948
Founds La Fundación Eva Perón, a charitable organization created in response to her rejection from the Sociedad de Beneficencia, which was run by women from Argentina high society

January 9, 1950
Faints during an official function. Taken to the hospital for an appendectomy and is diagnosed with cervical cancer three days later

1952
Publishes *La Razón de mi vida*, an autobiography covering her life from when she became First Lady in 1946 to 1952

June 4, 1952
Last public appearance

July 26, 1952
Dies in Buenos Aires at 33 years of age. Her body lies in view for 13 days while throngs of mourners wait in lines for up to 15 hours to pass by the casket

EVA PERÓN

The legendary status of Eva

Perón is confirmed by the many titles—official and unofficial—she has been given: Spiritual Leader of the Nation; Woman with the Whip; Santa Evita; Argentine Wonder Woman.

Born María Eva Ibarguen, she was the youngest child of Juana Ibarguen and a married rancher Juan Duarte, her mother's employer. Despite her father's wealth, the family lived in extreme poverty, exacerbated after his death in 1926. This experience influenced Eva's decision to leave home for Buenos Aires at 15 to pursue a career in the entertainment industry. There she became known as Eva Duarte. She modeled, acted on stage, and had minor roles in movies. Despite the charisma for which she became well known in her role as First Lady, she was a weak presence on the screen. Far more successful was her career in radio, in which she capitalized on her ability to express drama and emotion through her voice—a talent that she would later channel into fiery speeches in support of her husband.

Her poor beginnings influenced her political views and her advocacy for "los descamisados"—literally "the shirtless ones," but more generally a reference to poor, working-class Argentines. She was also a strong advocate for women's rights. She not only founded and served as president of the Female Perónist Party, she was also a tireless promoter of women's suffrage. When women were given the right to vote in 1947, she was the first to cast a ballot in an election. When she died of cervical cancer in 1952 aged 33, the nation came to a standstill.

Her first major "reappearance" was in the rock opera concept album *Evita*, penned by Tim Rice and Andrew Lloyd Webber and released in 1976—ironically the same year as the military coup that overthrew the government of Perón's third wife, Isabel, who had become president after serving as Vice President during Peron's third presidency. *Evita* went on to play successfully in London's West End and on Broadway in the late 1970s and 1980s. In 1996, the show was turned into a movie musical starring Madonna and Antonio Banderas.

Eva Perón has been the subject of books, masters' theses, doctoral dissertations, and special issues of academic journals. There is a monument, a museum, and a foundation in her name, and an official website, www. evitaperon.org which houses an extensive archive of photographs. Eva Perón did not elicit neutral opinions in life or in death.

Jonathan T. Reynolds

THE CUBAN MISSILE CRISIS

the 30-second history

In October 1962, the United States and the Soviet Union came close to a nuclear war. Soviet Premier Nikita Khrushchev had deployed missiles in Cuba, directly threatening the United States. Khrushchev hoped the presence of these missiles would protect communist Cuba from a US invasion and strengthen his hand in negotiations over Berlin. President John F. Kennedy was not about to accept missiles so close to the United States. After Kennedy received definitive proof of the missiles in Cuba in mid-October, he formed a special committee in the White House known as ExComm to deal with the crisis. Rejecting military options as too provocative given the potential for nuclear war, Kennedy decided to impose a blockade on Cuba. Then, the world held its breath as it waited to see if Khrushchev would respect the blockade. The Soviet leader did, and both sides were given valuable time to step back from the brink and negotiate a resolution to the perilous situation. The diplomatic breakthrough came when Khrushchev agreed to withdraw the missiles in exchange for Kennedy's pledge not to invade Cuba. Kennedy also promised in secret to remove US Jupiter missiles from Turkey.

RELATED TOPICS
See also
HIROSHIMA
page 62

SOVIET DEFEAT IN
AFGHANISTAN
page 68

THE FALL OF THE
BERLIN WALL
page 150

3-SECOND BIOGRAPHIES
NIKITA KHRUSHCHEV
1894–1971
Russian of humble origins who became premier of the Soviet Union (1958–64)

JOHN F. KENNEDY
1917–63
American politician and 35th US President (1961–63)

FIDEL CASTRO
1926–
Cuban communist leader during the Cold War and beyond

30-SECOND TEXT
Kristopher Teters

3-SECOND THRASH
On receiving news that Soviet ships had stopped heading toward Cuba, Kennedy's Secretary of State, Dean Rusk, remarked: "We're eyeball to eyeball and I think the other fellow just blinked."

3-MINUTE THOUGHT
Relations between the Soviet Union and the United States improved in the wake of the Cuban Missile Crisis. In June 1963, Kennedy called for peace between the two superpowers, urging Americans to reconsider their Cold War attitudes and declaring "in the final analysis ... We all breathe the same air. We all cherish our children's future. And we are all mortal." In August, the Soviets and the Americans agreed to a nuclear test ban treaty.

October 16–28, 1962 was the closest the world came to facing full-scale nuclear war.

"I HAVE A DREAM"

the 30-second history

On August 28, 1963, Dr. Martin Luther King, Jr. stood on the steps of the Lincoln Memorial in Washington, D.C., and delivered his "I Have a Dream" speech to close to a quarter of a million people. This was the climax of the civil rights movement's March on Washington for Jobs and Freedom. In his speech, King reminded Americans of the long history of injustices that African-Americans had faced. He called on the country to end racial discrimination and segregation and promote the freedom and equality of all citizens: America needed finally to live up to the words of the Declaration of Independence. Those fighting for civil rights would not be satisfied until these objectives were achieved. King powerfully declared: they would not be content "until justice rolls down like water and righteousness like a mighty stream." The most memorable part of the speech was when King discussed his "Dream" for the future. He envisaged a country in which blacks and whites could live together in harmony and racism would be a thing of the past. King's soaring rhetoric, particularly his "Dream," inspired many Americans and helped awaken the moral conscience of the nation. In this single speech, King dramatically crystallized the hopes and goals of the civil rights movement.

3-SECOND THRASH
"I have a dream that my four little children will one day live in a nation where they will not be judged by the color of their skin but by the content of their character."

3-MINUTE THOUGHT
Martin Luther King's "I Have a Dream" speech was so significant that the United States commemorated its fiftieth anniversary in 2013. The ceremony, which was held at the Lincoln Memorial, featured speeches by President Barack Obama, former presidents Jimmy Carter and Bill Clinton, and King family members. Around 100,000 people attended the commemoration.

RELATED TOPICS
See also
THE LONG MARCH
page 76

STONEWALL
page 88

THE END OF APARTHEID
page 92

3-SECOND BIOGRAPHIES
MARTIN LUTHER KING, JR.
1929–68
African-American leader in the civil rights movement of the 1950s and 60s whose nonviolent protest campaigns helped end segregation and regain voting rights for African- Americans

JOHN LEWIS
1940–
Leader of the Student Nonviolent Coordinating Committee, who spoke before King's Dream speech

30-SECOND TEXT
Kristopher Teters

King declared the gathering "the greatest demon-stration for freedom in the history of the Nation."

THE YEAR OF THE BARRICADES

the 30-second history

The year 1968 saw a worldwide wave of protests, primarily staged by student organizations of the New Left. These students rejected what they saw as the acquiescence by the "Old Left" to the status quo of capitalism, bureaucracy, militarism, and political repression. Action took many forms. In France, month-long protests in May united students and labor unions in demonstrations and a general strike. In West Germany, protestors focused on the nation's history in the Second World War, calling for the removal of all government officials with ties to the former Nazi Party. Czechoslovakia's Prague Spring began with liberal reforms and ended with the invasion of the country by Soviet troops. The United States saw massive riots fueled in part by disillusionment in the face of several major assassinations, most recently that of Senator Robert F. Kennedy on June 6, 1968. Protests against the Vietnam War took place in Japan, Germany, and the United States, including five days of violent demonstrations at the Democratic National Convention in Chicago. Protests before the Summer Olympics in Mexico City resulted in the Tlatelolco Massacre, when government troops killed at least dozens, if not hundreds, of students. By the end of the year, hundreds of students had been killed or injured.

RELATED TOPICS
See also
"I HAVE A DREAM"
page 84

DEATH IN DALLAS
page 144

3-SECOND BIOGRAPHIES
ALEXANDER DUBČEK
1921–92
Leader of Czechoslovakia (1968–69), whose attempted reforms set off the Prague Spring

ABBOTT "ABBIE" HOFFMAN
1936–89
American activist who founded the Youth International Party ("Yippies")

EDSON LUÍS DE LIMA SOUTO
1950–68
Brazilian student killed by military police in Rio de Janeiro, sparking wide protest in Brazil

30-SECOND TEXT
Sara Patenaude

Soviet tanks crushed the Prague Spring, but in France students and workers brought the economy briefly to its knees.

3-SECOND THRASH
The Year of the Barricades shook the world with student-led protests and demonstrations across four continents.

3-MINUTE THOUGHT
Prior to the 1960s, universities in the United States acted in *loco parentis*—that is in place of the parents. Students were expected to abide by university rules regulating speech, dress, curfews, and association with members of the opposite sex. The 1961 Supreme Court case *Dixon v. Alabama* rejected university claims of control, establishing that university students were entitled to their constitutional rights of free speech and association, opening the door to an age of student protests and radical free expression.

STONEWALL

the 30-second history

In the early morning of June 28, 1969 plainclothes police officers entered the Stonewall Inn, a popular gay club in New York City's Greenwich Village. In the 1960s raids on establishments that welcomed homosexuals were routine in the US but this time the police were unprepared. While officers waited for patrol vehicles to arrive, the crowd outside the bar swelled and tension mounted. As the police attempted to leave the scene, spectators began to riot. The officers retreated into the Stonewall Inn, barricading themselves in until reinforcements arrived. In the ensuing confrontation 13 people were arrested. The crowd was dispersed but the following night, a throng gathered outside the Stonewall Inn that included homosexuals, neighborhood residents, and curious visitors. Initially jovial, the mood quickly changed as police arrived. Protests continued for several nights, reportedly drawing crowds of 500–1,000 people. Though not the first events of the gay rights movement, the Stonewall Riots marked an important turning point, serving as a rallying cry for homosexuals and their allies. Activist groups sprang up across the United States, vocally demanding rights for gays and lesbians, and a year later the first gay pride marches marked the anniversary of the Stonewall Riots.

3-SECOND THRASH
A week of protests in 1969 transformed the Mafia-run Stonewall Inn from a local homosexual hotspot to the catalyst of the modern gay rights movement.

3-MINUTE THOUGHT
Being openly gay in the United States during the Cold War was not only illegal, it was also considered a threat to America—homosexuality was medically defined as a mental illness. Government officials feared that being gay left people open to the possibility of blackmail by communists. At the same time as Senator Joseph McCarthy's witch hunt for communists in the United States government, dozens of homosexual men were forced to resign their government posts.

RELATED TOPICS
See also
"I HAVE A DREAM"
page 84

THE YEAR OF THE
BARRICADES
page 86

THE END OF APARTHEID
page 92

THE PILL
page 124

3-SECOND BIOGRAPHIES
SYLVIA RIVERA
1951–2002
Founding member of the Gay Liberation Front

CRAIG RODWELL
1940–93
American gay rights activist and organizer of the first New York City gay pride march

30-SECOND TEXT
Sara Patenaude

After Stonewall, activists took to the streets in support of gay rights; the rainbow flag becoming a symbol of the community's diversity.

ARGENTINA'S DIRTY WAR

the 30-second history

Since declaring independence in 1816, Argentina has endured several periods of violence and rule by authoritarian governments. A military coup in 1976 initiated one of the most ferocious regimes, led by a group of generals known as "La Junta" who dubbed their policy the "Process of National Reorganization." The Junta, tacitly supported by the United States, initially targeted left-wing groups who had waged a guerrilla war against the government since the 1960s. The government's strategy was known as the "Dirty War"—using kidnapping, torture, rape, and disappearances as weapons against rebels, trade unionists, teachers, students, journalists, and others who were suspected of holding leftist sympathies: 10,000–30,000 "disappeared" during the seven years the Junta was in power. In 1977, the Mothers of the Plaza de Mayo movement, consisting of 14 mothers of the disappeared, began to hold weekly peaceful protests on the plaza of that name in Buenos Aires. When Britain defeated Argentina in the Falklands War in 1982, the Junta's dictatorship ended and democratic elections were held. This resulted in the election of a civilian, Raúl Alfonsín, in 1983. The new President created the National Commission on the Disappeared to investigate the disappearances.

RELATED TOPICS
See also
EVA PERÓN
page 80

THE CUBAN MISSILE CRISIS
page 82

THE YEAR OF THE BARRICADES
page 86

3-SECOND BIOGRAPHIES

AZUCENA VILLAFLOR
1924–77
Key founder of the Mothers of the Plaza de Mayo movement

RODOLFO WALSH
1927–77
Investigative journalist and member of the Montoneros movement

RAÚL ALFONSÍN
1927–2009
First democratically elected president of Argentina following the dictatorship

30-SECOND TEXT
Caryn Connelly

General Jorge Rafael Videla seized power in the 1976 coup and gave orders for gruesome tactics in the Dirty War.

3-SECOND THRASH
During the Dirty War in Argentina (1976–83), the military government committed atrocities against civilians in the attempt to rid the country of "subversive elements."

3-MINUTE THOUGHT
Argentina's Dirty War was not an anomalous event in the region. As part of the broader US-backed fight against communism in the hemisphere, authoritarian regimes came into power in Bolivia, Brazil, Chile, Paraguay, and Uruguay between the 1950s and 1970s. These governments united efforts in 1975 under the name Operation Condor. In 1977–86, the Argentine military provided training and intelligence to right-wing authoritarian regimes in Central America as part of Operation Charly.

THE END OF APARTHEID

the 30-second history

Amandla! ("Power!") This rallying cry symbolizes the combination of domestic passive resistance campaigns and international political pressure alongside economic sanctions that ended apartheid, the South African policy of institutional racism, in 1994. Under apartheid legislation of 1948, Afrikaner Nationalists legally categorized non-Europeans into "Africans," "Coloreds," "Asians" (Indians), and "Chinese." Some would argue that apartheid had begun in 1652, when the first Europeans, the Dutch, arrived, displacing Africans from their land. While the African nationalist movement in South Africa began in the late 19th/early 20th century, the defiance campaign to end apartheid was launched in 1955, when the African National Congress (ANC) ratified the 1955 Freedom Charter. The government, claiming to fight communism, responded to public demonstrations with mass arrests, violence, and repression. Two massacres, Sharpeville (1960) and Soweto (1976), shocked the world with images of police shooting civilians, especially children. Mounting world pressure and civil unrest convinced President F.W. de Klerk to release ANC leader Nelson Mandela after his 27 years imprisonment. Apartheid officially ended in 1994, with the first universal suffrage election—one person, one vote—electing Mandela and the ANC to power.

RELATED TOPICS
See also
THE LONG MARCH
page 76

"I HAVE A DREAM"
page 84

3-SECOND BIOGRAPHIES
MOHANDAS GANDHI
1869–1948
Indian nationalist who developed passive resistance tactics adopted by the ANC

NELSON MANDELA
1918–2013
South African leader of the antiapartheid movement and first universally elected president of South Africa

FREDERIK WILLEM DE KLERK
1936–
South African President (1989–94) who helped end apartheid

30-SECOND TEXT
Grace Chee

3-SECOND THRASH
The antiapartheid movement in South Africa was part of a worldwide nationalist and pan-African movement to overthrow colonialism and institute democracy.

3-MINUTE THOUGHT
In introducing apartheid, which means "apart-ness," or "apart-hood," the National Party sought to prevent Europeans from intermingling with or marrying other "races." To this end the government segregated economic, residential, and public social space. It enforced pass laws to control people's movements, legislated racial categories and economic distinctions, and forced African relocation to Bantustans (homelands) and townships, such as Soweto. Apartheid's economic legacies still linger.

The new South African flag combines the colors of the old regime with the yellow, black, and gold of the ANC.

INDUSTRY & ECONOMICS

INDUSTRY & ECONOMICS
GLOSSARY

"Big Box" stores This term refers to large retail establishments and chains that seek to capture a certain segment of the economy by selling large volumes at very low margins of profit. Due to their market dominance, they are often also referred to as "category killers" for their ability to overwhelm all forms of competition.

Black Thursday The day of October 24, 1929 is often referred to as "Black Thursday" because this is when the US stock market began its crash and the country started its slide into the Great Depression—dragging much of the global economy down with it.

Bolshevik Revolution Also known as the Great October Socialist Revolution, this event in October 1917, featured the overthrow by the Bolsheviks (one wing of the Russian Social-Democratic Workers' Party) of the moderate elements who had ruled Russia in the months since the ousting of the Tsarist monarchy in February 1917.

Collectivization With the end of the New Economic Policy in 1928, Joseph Stalin, leader of the Soviet Union, ordered the collectivization of peasant agricultural lands into state-run and managed farms. Despite popular discontent and poor agricultural performance, collectivized farms were a common component of statist economic policy around the world during much of the 20th century.

Dow Jones Industrial Index Often known simply as "the Dow," this index offers continuously updated information regarding the value of a set of 30 benchmark stocks. The Dow is one of the most closely watched indicators of the health of the American and global economy.

"Mom & Pop" stores This is an often nostalgic reference to the sort of small, family-owned retail and grocery establishments that were often driven out of business by larger chains and "Big Box" stores in the course of the 20th century.

New Economic Policy In 1921, the Soviet administration adopted an economic system of mixed private and public ownership in the New Economic Policy. The system allowed the private ownership of small companies and farms, while maintaining state control over large industrial and financial concerns.

Statism The belief that the state should have control of economic and/or social policies.

Wall Street Located in Lower Manhattan in New York City, Wall Street is the home to the New York Stock Exchange, the world's largest stock exchange. The term "Wall Street" is also used as a generic reference for American investment and financial institutions.

MODEL T FORD

the 30-second history

Henry Ford's Model T was the first mass-produced American automobile engineered and manufactured by the Ford Motor Company in Detroit. Made between 1908 and 1927, its moving assembly-line style of production used standard interchangeable parts and greatly reduced costs of production and maintenance, for the first time putting automobile ownership within reach of the average person. Model T production widened the impact of the industrial era, altered labor conditions for millions, and shaped popular culture around the world. More than 15 million Model Ts were eventually manufactured and sold worldwide. Popularly called the Tin Lizzie, the original Model T had no roof. Its wheels were wooden and its body was forged from a lightweight steel alloy. The car was operated using three foot-pedals and a lever on the driver's side. The lever on the steering wheel controlled the throttle—maximum speed was 45 mph. At the peak of efficiency, each automobile took one hour and 33 minutes to produce. The Model T's affordability imprinted a new cultural era with greater mobility and spurred government investment in the world's factories and highways. By the mid-1920s, half the cars in the world were Model Ts.

3-SECOND THRASH

The automobile became a symbol of economic prosperity: "A chicken in every pot and a car in every garage" was Herbert Hoover's 1928 Presidential campaign slogan.

3-MINUTE THOUGHT

Ever since the Model T, the world has been living on wheels. The Ford Motor Company was among the first successful multinational corporations. Versions of the Model T were produced on every continent, with factories in 12 countries. Without this popular automobile, there would have been no Route 66, no suburbia, no drive-in movies, and no fast-food chains. As with almost any invention, there were also negative consequences, including the global dependence on fossil fuel.

RELATED TOPIC

See also
"PILE IT HIGH, SELL IT LOW"
page 104

3-SECOND BIOGRAPHIES

KARL FRIEDRICH BENZ
1844–1929
German inventor of the automobile, the Benz Patent Motorwagen (1886)

HENRY FORD
1863–1947
American industrialist founder of the Ford Motor Company

30-SECOND TEXT

Candice Goucher

Henry Ford famously said customers could have the Model T in "any color so long as it is black," but in fact in 1908–14 the Model T was produced in gray, green, blue, and red.

FIVE YEAR PLANS

the 30-second history

Following the Bolshevik

Revolution, Lenin's new Soviet government implemented the New Economic Policy (NEP), which sought to balance state control over large economic concerns against peasant control of agricultural surpluses and the pursuit of profits by small businesses. With Lenin's death and Stalin's assumption of power in 1927, the limited freedoms of the NEP were dropped and the first Five Year Plan was announced. Through collectivization and state direction, the Plan called for industrial output to more than double in five years and for agricultural output to increase by 50 percent. Under the Plan the number of Soviet citizens employed in industry more than doubled, and industrial output surged, though it fell short of targets. Agricultural output, however, dropped drastically. In response, Stalin used the food shortage as a weapon against agricultural workers, whom he believed had sabotaged production. In Ukraine alone, between two and five million peasants starved to death in the 1930s. News of the famine was suppressed. Given its apparent success, which helped turn the Soviet Union into a world power, the Five Year Plan became a popular tool for rapid development elsewhere in the world, in states as diverse as China, Argentina, India, and Ghana.

3-SECOND THRASH
In 1928, the Soviet Union launched its first "Five Year Plan" and, for decades after, such plans were hallmarks of state-directed drives for development and prosperity.

3-MINUTE THOUGHT
The first Soviet Five Year Plan aimed to use centralized planning and careful allocation of resources rapidly to transform the USSR from peasant agricultural economy to modern industrial power. This effort featured the collectivization of agriculture and the creation of massive mining and manufacturing centers.

RELATED TOPICS
See also
SPUTNIK
page 24

THE WALL STREET CRASH
page 102

THE NEW DEAL
page 108

THE VOLTA DAM
page 110

THE CULTURAL REVOLUTION
page 142

3-SECOND BIOGRAPHIES
VLADIMIR ILYCH LENIN
1870–1924
First Premier of the Soviet Union

JOSEPH STALIN
1878–1953
Second Premier of the Soviet Union

30-SECOND TEXT
Jonathan T. Reynolds

Propaganda images promoted hard work in the service of Five Year Plans as heroic labor.

THE WALL STREET CRASH

the 30-second history

3-SECOND THRASH
In the fall of 1929, America's "Roaring Twenties" came to an end as a stock market crash dragged the US into a global depression.

3-MINUTE THOUGHT
On Black Thursday, the banks decided to pour money into the market in an attempt to save it. Their chosen representative, Richard Whitney, placed a huge bid on US Steel and several smaller bids on reliable stocks, a tactic that had worked in an earlier financial crash, in 1907. It slowed the decline … until Monday. Financial giants like the Rockefellers purchased huge amounts of stocks in an attempt to sway the public, but the panic and pandemonium proved unstoppable.

The Twenties. War was over, the economy booming. But it would not—could not—last. The first signs of trouble came in spring 1929. Several big industries saw production and sales slow; unemployment rates were already increasing. Meanwhile, the American public was eager to speculate, taking out bank loans to play the stock market. The Dow Jones Industrial Average reached its peak on September 3. The market wavered until October 24—Black Thursday—then began to fall, creating panic. Bankers attempted to stabilize the market, and President Hoover tried to reassure Americans. On Friday, it looked like things might improve, but on Monday, more trouble. By Tuesday, October 29, the market crashed. The United States and the world fell into depression, shaking public faith in capitalism. President Hoover believed in rugged individualism—the idea that people should succeed on their own with little interference from the government; ergo, he was slow to interfere. Eventually, he imposed higher taxes on imports to protect US farmers and businesses. He also lowered taxes. He instigated the building of the Colorado Dam to provide jobs and provided billions of dollars of aid. But still nothing jump-started the economy—until Franklin D. Roosevelt took office with promises of a New Deal.

RELATED TOPICS
See also
"PILE IT HIGH, SELL IT LOW"
page 104

JOHN MAYNARD KEYNES
page 106

FIVE YEAR PLANS
page 100

THE NEW DEAL
page 108

3-SECOND BIOGRAPHIES
HERBERT HOOVER
1874–1964
American engineer and humanitarian; 31st president of the United States (1929–33)

RICHARD WHITNEY
1888–1974
American financier; President of the New York Stock Exchange (1930–5)

30-SECOND TEXT
Kristin Hornsby

The Great Depression struck—investments collapsed, jobs disappeared, and a hungry people despaired.

"PILE IT HIGH, SELL IT LOW"

the 30-second history

After years working in retail stores A&P, Mutual Grocery, and Kroger, Michael J. Cullen developed the idea of selling larger volumes at lower prices. He proposed the scheme to the owner of Kroger, but his letter went unanswered. He leased a large automotive garage in Queens and in 1930 he opened the first "King Kullen." His supermarket built upon previous innovations, such as Piggly Wiggly's "self-service" shopping, but added the innovation of significantly lower prices and a huge level of choice. The store was an immediate hit, attracting customers from miles away, thanks to its car-friendly design. By launching in the early years of the Great Depression, Cullen capitalized on the need for cheaper foodstuffs. By 1936 Cullen had 16 additional stores, devastating other grocery operators. Cullen embraced his chain's reputation as the World's Greatest Price Wrecker; unable to compete, most "Mom & Pop" establishments went out of business. Existing chains, such as A&P (the Atlantic and Pacific Teas Co.) and Kroger, were able to adapt by adding larger stores that copied King Kullen's recipe for greater volume and profits. The process set in motion a commercial arms race of growing size and volume with lower prices that has continued to the present day.

3-SECOND THRASH
Promising to "Pile it High, Sell it Low," entrepeneur Michael J. Cullen transformed how the world buys its groceries.

3-MINUTE THOUGHT
In the early 20th century, grocery stores tended to be small and to serve a neighborhood. Many specialized, selling baked goods, or fruits and vegetables, or meat. Shopping meant visits to several locations and prices were high because operators needed to earn a living on relatively low volumes of sales. By launching a large establishment with a wide variety of foods and ample free parking, Michael Cullen invented the supermarket.

RELATED TOPICS
See also
THE WALL STREET CRASH
page 102

THE NEW DEAL
page 108

3-SECOND BIOGRAPHIES
MICHAEL J. CULLEN
1884–1936
Entrepreneur and inventor of the American supermarket

GEORGE LUDLUM HARTFORD
1864–1957
Chairman and treasurer of A&P who oversaw the shift from small groceries to supermarkets

JOHN EDWARD COHEN
1898–1979
Founder of the UK's Tesco supermarket chain

30-SECOND TEXT
Jonathan T. Reynolds

The first King Kullen, at 171st St. and Jamaica Ave. in Queens opened on August 4, 1930. Sales were cash only, and there was no delivery.

June 5, 1883
Born in Cambridge, England

1897
Awarded a scholarship to Eton College

1902
Enrols at King's College, Cambridge. Becomes active in the College Debating Society and later serves as its president

1906
Begins work at the India Office of the Civil Service in London

1913
Publishes his first book, *Indian Currency and Finance*

1914–18
Works for the British Treasury

1919
His second work, *The Economic Consequences of the Peace*, is published

1924
Becomes First Bursar of King's College, Cambridge

1925
Marries Russian ballerina Lydia Lopokova

1929
Becomes a Fellow of the British Academy

1936
His magnum opus, *The General Theory of Employment, Interest, and Money*, is published

1937
Becomes director of the British Eugenics Society

1939–45
Serves as a British representative to the US in negotiating financial support for Britain's war effort (a role he also performed in the First World War)

April 21, 1946
Dies in Sussex, England

JOHN MAYNARD KEYNES

John Maynard Keynes was born to a prominent English family. As a child he impressed his teachers with his intuitive grasp of mathematics and frustrated them with his intellectual independence. He attended Eton College and established himself as one of that prestigious institution's top students. In 1902 he was accepted to King's College, Cambridge University, where he excelled in economics and distinguished himself as a speaker and debater.

In 1906 Keynes took a position with the Revenue, Statistics, and Commerce section of the British Civil Service India Office. Though he resigned his position in 1908, his time in the India Office was clearly influential, reflected in his first book *Indian Currency and Finance* (1913). Over the next years he undertook a number of professional activities, ranging from lecturing part-time at Cambridge to publishing articles in influential magazines and serving as editor for the scholarly *Economics Journal*.

With the outbreak of the First World War, Keynes was enlisted by the British Treasury Department to help set economic policy during the war. By 1917 he had been given responsibility for negotiating key financial elements of the allied war effort. After the end of hostilities, Keynes was outspoken in his condemnation of the heavy reparations levied on Germany, eventually authoring *The Economic Consequences of the Peace* (1919).

In the same year he was the Treasury's financial representative at the Paris Peace Conference in Versailles.

During the late 1920s, as Europe slid into economic depression, Keynes began to challenge the British government's laissez-faire economics and argued for such radical notions as lowering of interest rates and using government spending to stimulate economies. These ideas greatly influenced Roosevelt's New Deal policies in the US and eventually became the basis of Keynes' *General Theory of Employment, Interest, and Money* (1936)— widely held to be the most influential economics text of the 20th century.

With the rise of fascism, Keynes called for a stand against Italian and German aggression. When war broke out in 1939, he returned to his role as a British negotiator. He made repeated visits to the US, the most significant of which was his attendance of the Bretton Woods talks, a gathering in July 1944 of representatives of the Second World War allies to determine international monetary policy for the postwar years. The strenuous nature of the negotiations, however, took a toll on his health. He suffered a series of heart attacks during the period from 1944 to 1946, eventually succumbing on April 21, 1946.

Jonathan T. Reynolds

THE NEW DEAL

the 30-second history

Amid the Great Depression, in
1932 Democrat Franklin Roosevelt won the US
presidency. He immediately instituted a sweeping
domestic agenda termed the New Deal. During
the first 100 days of his administration he signed
into law a staggering amount of legislation to aid
the country's economic recovery. This legislation
created numerous federal agencies to regulate
the economy and provide jobs for the large
numbers of unemployed people in the United
States. For example, the Civilian Conservation
Corps put people to work conserving and
developing America's natural resources,
particularly its national parks. The Civil Works
Administration employed millions in improving
infrastructure. Beyond providing immediate relief
for the unemployed, Roosevelt wanted to give
people economic security. The Social Security Act
of 1935 helped meet this goal by establishing a
federal pension system for the elderly and
providing unemployment insurance and aid to
families with dependent children. The act marked
the rise of the welfare state in the United States.
Ultimately, the New Deal did not pull the US out
of the Depression, but it helped alleviate the
suffering of millions of people and drive down
the unemployment rate. Additionally, the federal
government assumed greater responsibility for
the economy and the well-being of Americans.

3-SECOND BIOGRAPHIES
FRANKLIN D. ROOSEVELT
1882–1945
32nd President of the United
States who led America
through the Great Depression
and the Second World War

FRANCES PERKINS
1880–1965
American civil servant, staunch
New Dealer, the first woman
to serve in a president's
cabinet, and Roosevelt's
Secretary of Labor (1933–45)

30-SECOND TEXT
Kristopher Teters

*Franklin D. Roosevelt's
New Deal aimed to get
Americans back to
work in the face of the
Great Depression.*

Work Pays America!

PROSPERITY

WORKS PROGRESS ADMINISTRATION

THE VOLTA DAM

the 30-second history

3-SECOND THRASH
Ghana's Volta Dam
epitomizes persistent
underdevelopment; its
technological promises
fell short by supplying
electricity to foreign
manufacturers, leaving
locals in the dark.

3-MINUTE THOUGHT
Ghana's first president,
Kwame Nkrumah, wanted
to use the dam project to
build a modern industrial
state. With local
hydroelectric power, he
hoped to turn 200 million
tons of Ghanaian bauxite
into aluminum. Instead,
Nkrumah was forced to
rely on costly loans and
deals with multinational
corporations to fund the
project. Kaiser Aluminum
processed imported
bauxite using the dam's
cheap electricity; Nkrumah
was overthrown in a coup
engineered by the
United States.

The Akosombo Dam was built
between 1961 and 1965 on the Volta River in the
West African nation of Ghana. Constructed to
deliver hydroelectric power, the dam led to the
displacement of more than 80,000 Ghanaians.
Its reservoir, Lake Volta, became the world's
largest human-made lake, covering about 3,283
square miles (8,052 square km). Plans to dam
the river existed as early as 1915, at the height
of the colonial era. During the fight for African
independence and subsequent struggles for
economic sovereignty, big dams symbolized
modernity—yet few delivered all they promised.
The Volta valley inundation destroyed 700
villages and altered the region's ecology. Funded
by the World Bank and British and American
governments, the hydroelectric power plant sold
electricity to foreign aluminum companies; only
about 20 percent of the electricity eventually
benefitted local people, who continued to
endure rolling blackouts and power cuts. The
Akosombo Dam helped Ghana to industrialize
and today industry accounts for about one
quarter of total GDP. The hydroelectric plant
continues to supply an aluminum smelter at
the city of Tema and excess power is sold to
neighboring countries. In 2007, the Sinohydro
Corporation of China was contracted to build
a second dam at Bui.

RELATED TOPIC
See also
RED RUBBER SCANDAL IN THE
BELGIAN CONGO
page 136

3-SECOND BIOGRAPHIES
HENRY J. KAISER
1882–1967
American industrialist,
consulting engineer on the
Volta Dam Project and owner
of Kaiser Aluminum

KWAME NKRUMAH
1909–72
Ghana's first president and
proponent of the Volta Dam
Project

30-SECOND TEXT
Candice Goucher

*Despite displacing
thousands of people
and impacting
negatively on the
environment, the
dam did not deliver
for local people.*

THE ARAB OIL EMBARGO

the 30-second history

On the Jewish holy day of Yom Kippur in 1973, Egypt and Syria, supported by other Arab states, launched a coordinated attack on Israel. The unexpected strike initially drove back the defenders, but with significant US military aid, the Israelis eventually regained territory, with the war ending largely in a stalemate. In response, Arab petroleum exporters sought to punish the United States and other Western powers by announcing on October 16 a 70 percent increase in the price of crude oil. Additional price increases, and reductions in the volume of exports, followed. As a result, the price of oil increased from roughly $3 per barrel to $12 per barrel in only six months. In some markets petroleum prices doubled. The world economy, already shaken by the United States dropping the gold standard and pulling out of the Bretton Woods agreement of 1944, was in turmoil. Stock markets crashed and industrial economies around the world stalled and fell into recession. The American car industry, which focused on large fuel-hungry vehicles, was forced to retool. Developing economies were also hard-hit, as the cost of imported fuel overwhelmed limited national budgets.

3-SECOND THRASH
In 1973, the world was thrown into recession when Arab oil producers deployed what they called the "oil weapon."

3-MINUTE THOUGHT
Following the Yom Kippur War of October 6–26, 1973, Arab oil producers launched an embargo of Western nations who had supported Israel during the conflict. Over the course of six months, the cost of oil jumped more than 400 percent, resulting in much higher petroleum prices and fuel shortages around the world. Oil-producing countries, however, underwent an "oil boom." Only in the 1980s did the wider world economy begin to recover.

RELATED TOPICS
See also
THE FIRST ARAB–ISRAELI WAR
page 64

THE WALL STREET CRASH
page 102

30-SECOND TEXT
Jonathan T. Reynolds

The sudden spike in oil prices had many effects, including introduction of a national speed limit of 55mph (89kmph) in the United States, to save fuel.

MEDICINE & HEALTH

Antiretroviral Drugs/HAART These drugs represent a class of antiviral medicines designed to attack and inhibit different stages of retroviral infection and replication. When several of these drugs are used in combination to treat HIV (the Human Immunodeficiency Virus), this process is known as Highly Active Anti-Retroviral Therapy.

DNA Deoxyribonucleic acid provides the basic building block of all life on Earth. It takes the form of a polymer chain made up of nucleotides arranged in the form of a double helix, each side contains an identical code. Each organism's DNA is linked together in the form of genes and chromosomes.

Human Genome Project Launched in 1990, this project sought to identify the location and function of the 3.3 billion base pairs of genetic data found within the human genetic code. Completed in 2003, the project has revolutionized our understanding of human diversity, disease, and evolution.

Pandemic A pandemic refers to a disease epidemic that has infected a very large area—several countries, continents, or the entire world. Examples include: the flu pandemic of 1918–19; the HIV pandemic that began in the 1980s; and the SARS pandemic of 2002–03.

SARS Probably originating in a disease hosted by wild animals such as civits, racoon dogs, and bats, the virus causing the Severe Acute Respiratory Syndrome made the zoonotic jump to human populations in southern China in 2002 and then spread to 37 additional countries during the following year. Fatality rates for infected persons reached nearly 10 percent.

Zoonosis Most diseases do not strike a single species. The process of a disease jumping from one species to another, particularly from animals to humans, is known as *zoonosis*. Sometimes, but not always, this transmission may require a mutation to take place in the infectious agent.

SPANISH FLU

the 30-second history

Influenza outbreaks have been a fact of human life for centuries, especially in temperate regions. Worldwide, flu kills tens of thousands of people annually. Between 1918 and 1920, however, a triple wave of particularly virulent influenza outbreaks killed tens of millions. One of the early outbreaks was in Fort Riley, Kansas, from where flu spread as troops were mobilized for combat in Europe. Wartime governments were hesitant to impose quarantines or issue health warnings for fear of undermining the war effort. Indeed, the name Spanish Flu reflected the fact that neutral Spain did not censor news of the flu. During spring 1918 the first wave of infections spread rapidly but were no more deadly than usual flu outbreaks. During the following fall and winter, however, a new, more deadly strain of the virus emerged—one that not only endangered the young and old but also, unusually, struck young adults. The 1918 outbreak was also unusual in that it spread to tropical regions where flu is rare. The demobilization of troops, many of whom had been drafted from European colonies in Africa and Asia, facilitated the spread of the outbreak. In the 1990s the 1918 pandemic was identified as an H1N1 variety of the flu.

3-SECOND THRASH
This influenza pandemic killed more people in two years than did the infamous Bubonic Plague over many centuries.

3-MINUTE THOUGHT
Though it was named Spanish Flu, this catastrophic influenza epidemic's exact origin has never been determined. The infection seems to have appeared almost simultaneously in North America, Europe, and Asia. The spread of the disease was facilitated by the movement of troops and supplies during the First World War. Perhaps a third of the world's population was infected. This particular influenza was unusually virulent: 3–5 percent of the population—between 50 and 100 million people—perished.

RELATED TOPICS
See also
SLOPPY PETRI DISH
page 120

ERADICATION OF SMALLPOX
page 128

HIV/AIDS
page 130

3-SECOND BIOGRAPHIES
RUPERT BLUE
1868–1948
American Surgeon-General during the outbreak

JOHN SYDNEY OXFORD
1942–
British virologist who has studied the 1918 flu epidemic

30-SECOND TEXT
Jonathan T. Reynolds

The flu spread quickly among troops living at close quarters, men who were moved from country to country by the demands of the First World War.

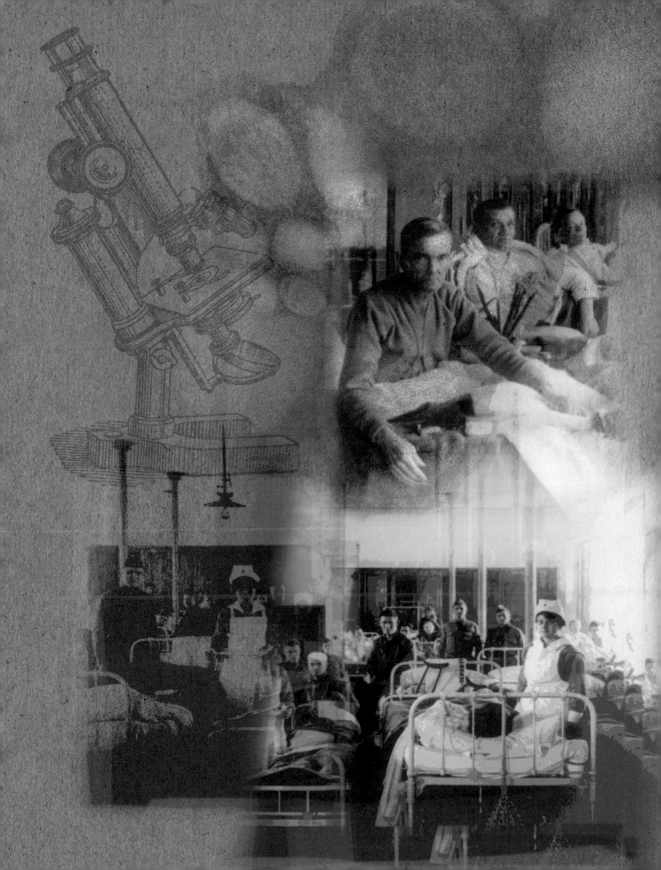

SLOPPY PETRI DISH

the 30-second history

In 1921 scientist Alexander Fleming accidentally discovered the antibacterial substance lysozyme when his runny nose dripped into a Petri dish of bacteria. A few years later, the world again benefitted from Fleming's sloppy Petri dish handling. In 1928 Fleming went on vacation, leaving Petri dishes containing *Staphylococcus aureus* on his workbench. On his return, Fleming found that mold had contaminated several of the dishes. One of these molds had killed the *Staphylococcus* bacterium. Upon further examination, the mold was found to be nontoxic and effective at killing a large variety of bacteria. It was not until 1940 that Howard Florey and Ernst Chain found a way to isolate the penicillin from the mold and produce it in a form useful to those who were ill. Mass production of penicillin quickly followed and the drug was sent to the battlefronts during the Second World War, saving countless lives from deadly infections. In the ensuing decades, the widespread use of antibiotics significantly reduced death and debilitation from sources ranging from small wounds to dental infections to sexually transmitted diseases. Perhaps only the eradication of smallpox compares as a triumph over illness in human history.

RELATED TOPICS
See also
SPANISH FLU
page 118

ERADICATION OF SMALLPOX
page 128

3-SECOND BIOGRAPHIES
ALEXANDER FLEMING
1881–1955
British bacteriologist and discoverer of penicillin

HOWARD FLOREY
1898–1968
Australian pharmacologist and pathologist who assisted in the production of usable penicillin

ERNST CHAIN
1906–79
German biochemist who assisted in the production of usable penicillin

30-SECOND TEXT
Sara Patenaude

3-SECOND THRASH
We all have Alexander Fleming's sloppy handling of his Petri dishes to thank for one of the greatest medical discoveries of the modern age.

3-MINUTE THOUGHT
The most common cause of death in wartime was not bullets, but the resulting infections of the wounds they caused. Wartime conditions also increased the likelihood of diseases including influenza, cholera, and typhus. With the discovery and mass-manufacture of penicillin, wounded soldiers were much more likely to survive the war and return to their families. The Allied forces in the Second World War saw these advantages and supported the production of penicillin as a war industry.

Fleming shared the 1945 Nobel Prize for Physiology with Howard Florey and Ernst Chain, who developed penicillin as a drug for wide use.

DOUBLE HELIX

the 30-second history

The term "double helix" describes the three-dimensional structure of DNA (deoxyribonucleic acid), the molecule that encodes the genetic instructions found in the cells of all living things. The discovery of the double helix shape—like a ladder whose opposite ends are turned to twist the rungs into a sprial—helped unlock the basis of mutations (genetic changes) and replication (transmission of inherited characteristics) in the history of life. DNA was actually discovered in the 19th century by a Swiss researcher, Friedrich Miescher. For more than half a century other scientists struggled to imagine how the protein-coded DNA worked to take the information in the cell and transmit those instructions to make specific proteins. In 1953, Francis Crick, James Watson, and Maurice Wilkins were credited with being the first to unlock the structural arrangement of DNA's components or building blocks as linked pairs. They shared the Nobel Prize in 1962. Visualizing the structure of DNA enabled a generation of scientists to describe how genetics worked to pass information from parent to offspring and paved the way for the Humane Genome Project, which sought to sequence and map all the genes of the human body.

RELATED TOPICS
See also
THE THEORY OF RELATIVITY
page 14

SLOPPY PETRI DISH
page 120

ROSALIND FRANKLIN
page 126

3-SECOND BIOGRAPHIES
FRANCIS CRICK
1916–2004
British physicist

MAURICE WILKINS
1916–2004
New Zealand-born physicist and molecular biologist

ROSALIND FRANKLIN
1920–58
Pioneer British molecular biologist

JAMES D. WATSON
1928–
American molecular biologist

30-SECOND TEXT
Candice Goucher

3-SECOND THRASH
Although Crick and Watson did not discover DNA, their description of its double-helix structure has been heralded as the greatest scientific discovery of the 20th century.

3-MINUTE THOUGHT
Three men received the 1962 Nobel Prize for the discovery of DNA's structure. The Nobel committee overlooked Rosalind Franklin, whose photographs led to the discovery of DNA's shape. Her images of DNA molecules convinced Crick and Watson that their original structure was incorrect. Franklin's article appeared in an issue of *Nature* immediately following Crick and Watson's, the men were given "first place."

Crick and Watson were helped by Franklin to visualize DNA's spiraling double helix.

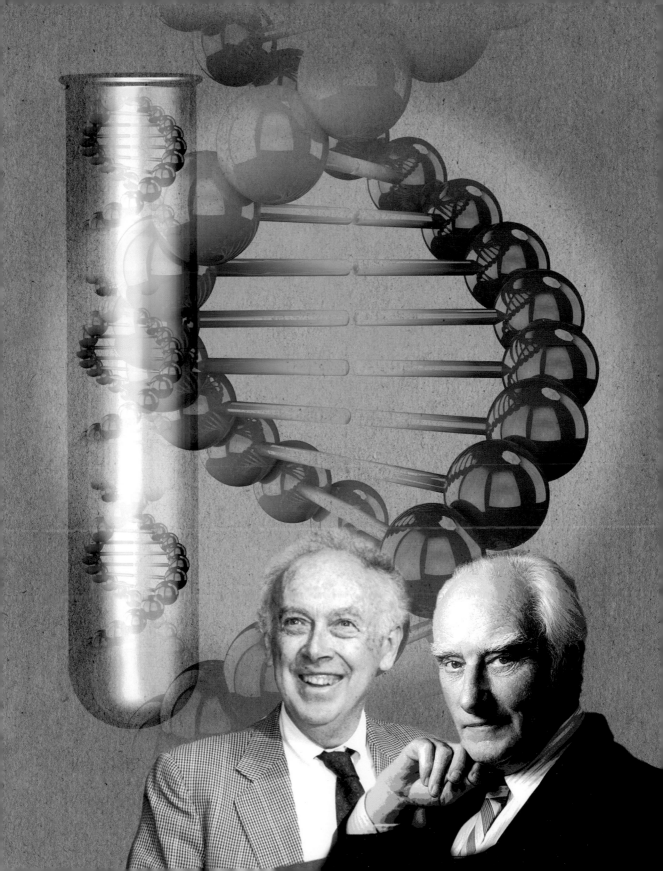

THE PILL

the 30-second history

The term "birth control" was first used in publication by Margaret Sanger in the June 1914 issue of her newsletter *The Woman Rebel*. At this time, birth control referred to methods of controlling pregnancy by timing sexual activity with a woman's menstrual cycle or using barrier-type contraceptives such as condoms and diaphragms. Sanger, a nurse, advocated these methods while holding out hope for a "magic pill" that women could take to prevent pregnancy safely. In her quest for such a pill, Sanger introduced scientist Gregory Pincus to philanthropist Katharine McCormick, who agreed to fund Pincus's research into an oral contraceptive method. Alongside John Rock, Pincus created a medication with progesterone, a naturally occurring hormone that regulates ovulation. Women who take progesterone do not ovulate, and thus cannot become pregnant. After extensive clinical testing, the Food and Drug Administration (FDA) approved use of the pill for women experiencing menstrual problems and, in 1960, extended approval for all women to use it as a contraceptive. By 1963, more than 2.3 million American women were taking the pill; a mere five years later the number of women using it jumped to more than 12 million worldwide even though it had been officially condemned by Pope Paul VI.

RELATED TOPICS
See also
HIV/AIDS
page 130

3-SECOND BIOGRAPHIES
MARGARET SANGER
1879–1966
American activist and founder of the American Birth Control League

GREGORY PINCUS
1903–67
American biologist, inventor of the birth control pill

JOHN ROCK
1890–1984
American obstetrician and head of clinical trials for the birth control pill

KATHARINE MCCORMICK
1875–1967
American biologist and benefactor who funded the research into oral contraception

30-SECOND TEXT
Sara Patenaude

Control over fertility revolutionized women's influence over their private and professional lives.

3-SECOND THRASH
The pill made it safe and easy for women to take control of their fertility.

3-MINUTE THOUGHT
Oral contraceptive pills remained controversial even after FDA approval. Many states prohibited any sales of the pill, leading to the 1965 Supreme Court case of *Griswold v. Connecticut*, which determined that states could not prohibit the use of birth control by married couples. The 1972 Supreme Court case *Eisenstadt v. Baird* extended this protection to unmarried women. Both cases used arguments of Constitutional rights to privacy and free association to win their suits.

July 25, 1920
Born in London, to a
well-to-do family

1931
Attends St. Paul's Girl's
School, London, and
shows talent for
chemistry and physics

1938–1941
Studies chemistry at
Newnham College,
Cambridge

1941
Awarded research
scholarship to work on
gas chromatography

1942–45
Gives up the scholarship
to work instead on the
microstructure of coal
for the British Coal
Utilisation Research
Association, work that
gains her a PhD from
Cambridge

1947
Takes job in Paris,
learning techniques of
X-ray diffraction

1951
Takes research associate
position at King's
College, London,
studying the structure
of deoxyribonucleic acid
(DNA) alongside Maurice
Wilkins and Raymond
Gosling

May 1952
Captures what is now
known as Photo 51

1953
Crick and Watson publish
their DNA model

1953
Franklin takes job at
Birkbeck College to study
the structure of
ribonucleic acid (RNA)

1956
Cancer is diagnosed

April 16, 1958
Dies in London from
ovarian cancer

1962
Francis Crick, James
Watson, and Maurice
Wilkins awarded the
Nobel Prize for their
work on the DNA model

ROSALIND FRANKLIN

Rosalind Franklin was a true innovator both in terms of science and of women working in what was traditionally a man's field. Determined to become a scientist, Franklin attended Cambridge University, to study physical chemistry as it related to coal, a vital wartime resource. This was the subject of the thesis for her PhD, which she earned in 1945.

In 1944, Franklin took a job in a Parisian laboratory with crystallographer Jacques Méring. Méring taught her X-Ray diffraction, and soon she was able to capture images of single crystals and chemical molecules.

In 1947, Franklin accepted a post as research associate at King's College, London, working alongside Maurice Wilkins with the assistance of PhD student Raymond Gosling. At King's she experienced workplace discrimination (for example, there was a men-only dining facility) and she and Wilkins often clashed. However, she worked diligently, fine-tuned her instruments, and, with the help of Gosling, captured a series of amazing photos of DNA, including one nicknamed Photo 51, which has been described as the most important photograph ever taken. She also tested the reactions of DNA fibers to various conditions, which aided her study of the structure of DNA.

In January 1953, Wilkins, without Franklin's knowledge, selected what is now her most famous photograph and showed it to his friend, American geneticist James Watson. Seeing Photo 51, a striped, cross-shape, enabled him to understand that DNA has a double-helix structure. Watson returned to his partner, Francis Crick, at Cambridge with the image, and their now-famous model of DNA was published two months later. Today we realize just how much influence Franklin had on the Watson-Crick model. Watson attended a 1951 lecture by Franklin in which she discussed two forms of DNA, form A and B, the latter of which was a helix; by 1953, she had concluded that both forms were double helices with backbones on the outside. Watson and Crick had many discussions with Franklin's lab partner, Wilkins, resulting in unauthorized access to information, such as Photo 51.

Franklin left King's College for Birkbeck College in 1953 to study the structure of RNA and viruses. She undertook a great deal of research on the tobacco mosaic virus and began work on the polio virus, but had grown ill and was diagnosed with ovarian cancer. On April 16, 1958 Rosalind Franklin died; she was 37.

In 1962, Crick, Watson, and Wilkins received the Nobel Prize in Physiology or Medicine for their work on the DNA model. It remains one of the most controversial Nobel Prizes awarded because its recipients excluded Rosalind Franklin. Technically, Franklin was not eligible, having died four years earlier; the Nobel Prize is not given posthumously. Only in recent years has the scope of her contribution been recognized.

Kristin Hornsby

ERADICATION
OF SMALLPOX

the 30-second history

Smallpox was an unusually
virulent infectious disease. Easily transmitted
by physical or airborne contact, the virus caused
puss-filled blisters, high fevers, and intense aches
and pains. Around 30 percent of adults and 80
percent of children infected died from
hemorrhaging caused by the disease. Survivors
were often terribly scarred. Outbreaks routinely
produced plague-like panics that helped to spread
the disease. Vaccination techniques were
independently developed in several world regions,
but widespread inoculation did not begin until
the 1800s. By the 1950s, global deaths had been
cut to a still staggering 2 million annually. Efforts
to eradicate the disease began in 1956 and were
expanded in 1966 with the creation of the
Smallpox Eradication Unit, involving health
specialists from around the world. The project
developed a system to identify and isolate
outbreaks as quickly as possible. The last
European outbreak of smallpox occurred in
Yugoslavia in 1972, with isolated instances of the
disease in India and east Africa in 1975 and 1977.
The last death from smallpox occurred after a lab
incident in Birmingham, UK, in 1978. In 1980, the
WHO declared smallpox eradicated. Despite calls
for the destruction of lab samples of the disease,
the United States and Russia have refused to
eliminate all specimens under their control.

RELATED TOPICS
See also
SPANISH FLU
page 118

SLOPPY PETRI DISH
page 120

HIV/AIDS
page 130

3-SECOND BIOGRAPHIES
FRANK JOHN FENNER
1914–2010
Australian microbiologist who
chaired the Global Commission
for the Certification of
Smallpox Eradication

JANET PARKER
1938–78
British medical photographer
and last person known to have
died of smallpox

30-SECOND TEXT
Jonathan T. Reynolds

3-SECOND THRASH
The eradication of
smallpox through an
international campaign
running from 1956 to 1980
is perhaps the greatest
achievement of the
20th century.

3-MINUTE THOUGHT
Smallpox may have been
the greatest infectious
killer in history. Outbreaks
occurred in Ancient Egypt,
and by the 16th century it
routinely killed 10–15
percent of every
generation. As late as the
1960s, it killed an
estimated 2 million people
per year, and perhaps as
many as 500 million over
the course of the 20th
century. In 1956 the World
Health Organization
launched a campaign to
eliminate the disease. By
1980 smallpox was
declared eradicated.

*Smallpox caused a very
unsightly rash with
blisters and in some
cases led to blindness
caused by scarring of
the cornea.*

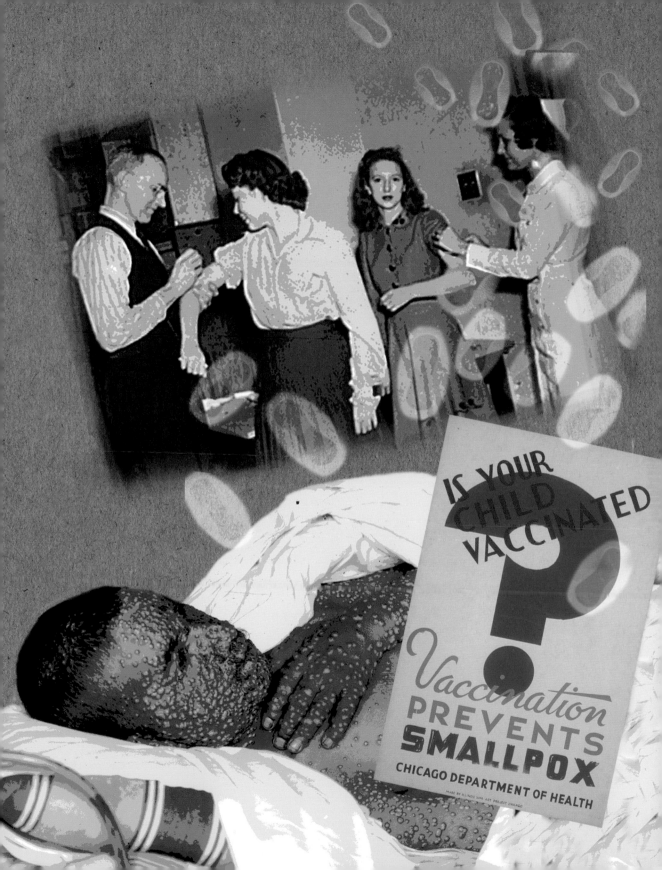

IS YOUR CHILD VACCINATED?

Vaccination PREVENTS SMALLPOX

CHICAGO DEPARTMENT OF HEALTH

HIV/AIDS

the 30-second history

HIV (Human Immunodeficiency Virus) causes AIDS (Acquired Immunodeficiency Syndrome). Early in the 20th century the disease had established a foothold in rapidly growing cities in parts of Africa and spread via several vectors, including sexual transmission, blood transfusions, and the reuse of needles during medical procedures. Long-distance labor migration to mines in central and southern Africa, where male miners had access to sex workers, likely hastened its spread. Internationally, two groups, hemophiliacs and homosexuals, were particularly vulnerable to early infection. Other sources of infection included blood transfusions, intravenous drug use, and unprotected sex. The identification of the virus by the Pasteur Institute in 1983, launched a search for treatments. Research into antiretroviral drugs eventually led to the development of Highly Active Antiretroviral Therapy (HAART), which by the 1990s proved capable of halting the infection's progression to AIDS. Drug patents, however, rendered these medications prohibitively expensive for the vast majority of those infected. International agreement in 1995 allowed countries facing medical crises to gain access to cheaper versions of the medications. Since the 1990s, education campaigns supporting safe sex, combined with the HAART regime, have helped reduce infection and death rates worldwide.

RELATED TOPICS
See also
SPANISH FLU
page 118

ERADICATION OF SMALLPOX
page 128

3-SECOND BIOGRAPHIES
LUC ANTOINE MONTAGNIER
1932–
French virologist who first identified the HIV virus

ROBERT CHARLES GALLO
1937–
American virologist who confirmed that HIV was responsible for AIDS

EARVIN "MAGIC" JOHNSON, JR.
1959–
American professional basketball player whose announcement of being HIV positive in 1991 helped "break the silence" and overcome the stigma associated with HIV

30-SECOND TEXT
Jonathan T. Reynolds

HIV was spread from primates to humans and then HIV/AIDS was transmitted swiftly and fatally around the world.

3-SECOND THRASH
First recognized as a viral disease in the early 1980s, HIV spread to become a global pandemic that had infected nearly 30 million people by 2000.

3-MINUTE THOUGHT
The HIV virus originally infected primate populations in Central and West Africa. The zoonosis event (transmission of the disease to humans) probably occurred in the process of hunting or butchering primates for food. Over decades, human migration spread the virus across Africa and, during the 1960s, individuals, probably crew members of merchant vessels, carried the disease to different parts of the world. Other virally spread diseases— including SARS and monkeypox—are also likely to have originated by cross-species transmission.

EVENTS, TRIUMPHS & TRAGEDIES

Charter of Paris for a New Europe (1990)
As the collapse of the Soviet system and Warsaw Pact became apparent, a summit was arranged to seek to reorganize relationships between Western and Eastern powers. The resulting Charter of Paris laid the groundwork for post-Cold War cooperation and crisis resolution among formerly hostile powers.

Cold War This term describes the competition between the United States and the Soviet Union from after the Second World War (1939–45) to the collapse of the Soviet Union in 1989–91. The term "Cold War" highlighted that the conflict was more about ideas and political allegiance among allies than about warfare. The Cold War was nonetheless very hot in places such as Korea, Angola, and Afghanistan.

The Final Solution Formally established in 1942, the Nazi strategy to "solve the Jewish question" was a euphemistic description of the shift in Nazi policy from the effort to subjugate and drive out Jewish populations to a determination to exterminate them.

Iron Curtain Though a popular metaphor before the Cold War, the term "Iron Curtain" came to describe the physical division between communist eastern Europe and capitalist western Europe after British prime minister Winston Churchill used it in a 1945 telegram to US President Harry Truman. These fences and walls were generally established to prevent eastern Europeans from fleeing into western Europe.

Maoism This term refers to the political, economic, and social theory developed and espoused by Chinese communist leader Mao Zedong. The Chinese Communist Party defines Maoism as "Marxism-Leninism applied in a Chinese context." Other core components included a strong degree of anti-Confucianism—opposition to the philosophical and ethical system based on the teachings of Chinese philosopher Confucius—and emphasis on peasant-based revolution.

North Atlantic Treaty Organization (NATO)
Established in 1949, this mutual defense pact provided a framework for defensive military coordination between most western European and North American states. Though initially designed to guard against potential Soviet expansion into western Europe, the organization expanded after the collapse of the Soviet Union.

Warren Commission Formally known as the Presidents Commission on the Assassination of President Kennedy. Under the leadership of Chief Justice Earl Warren, the commission determined that gunmen Lee Harvey Oswald and Jack Ruby had acted independently.

Warsaw Pact Formed in 1955, this mutual defense pact among eastern European communist states and the Soviet Union was a response to western Germany's entry into NATO. Following the collapse of the Soviet Union, several former Warsaw Pact states applied for NATO membership.

Zyklon-B gas Originally developed as a pesticide in the 1920s, this cyanide-based poison gas was used by Nazi Germany to murder an estimated 1.2 million people during the Holocaust. Most of the victims were Jewish. Some 200,000 of the killed were Polish and Soviet prisoners of war and Roma.

RED RUBBER SCANDAL IN THE BELGIAN CONGO

the 30-second history

3-SECOND THRASH
The Congo Free State's reliance on violence led to great loss of life and inspired an international human rights alliance to battle the regime's severe colonial injustices.

3-MINUTE THOUGHT
Africans as well as Westerners exposed the cruelty of the Congo Free State. In 1903 Herzekiah Shanu, a Nigerian photographer who worked for Leopold II's regime, sent damning evidence of the ruthlessness of colonial officials to Casement and Morel. A police officer discovered Shanu's secret role as an informant, and the colonial government refused to hire him again. Bankrupt and depressed, Shanu committed suicide in 1905.

In 1885 through diplomatic dealings Belgian king Leopold II had established the Congo Free State, a vast territory in central Africa, as his private property. The king granted concessions in his colony to unscrupulous companies. Booming demand for rubber from the nascent automobile industry at the turn of the 20th century led companies to plunder the Free State's natural resources and use intimidation tactics and violence against the Congolese to punish those who did not harvest enough of the prized latex. Leopold's government endorsed the razing of villages and mutilations. The atrocities were exposed by a group of Western activists including American author Mark Twain, British diplomat Roger Casement, and journalist E.D. Morel, who displayed photographs of Congolese people with severed hands to mock Leopold's claims that his colony promoted Christian civilization. The death toll from illness and violence may have been as high as several hundred thousand. The Congo reform movement helped to force Leopold to sell his colony to the Belgian government in 1908. The government proved to be more efficient than Leopold's regime, but often just as rapacious. One employee of Leopold's, Joseph Conrad, wrote the haunting novella *Heart of Darkness* based on his Congolese experiences. European conquest came at a brutal price.

RELATED TOPIC
See also
PATRICE LUMUMBA
page 146

3-SECOND BIOGRAPHIES
MARK TWAIN (SAMUEL L. CLEMENS)
1835–1910
American author and fierce critic of the US occupation of the Philippines and European imperialism in Africa

JOSEPH CONRAD
1857–1924
British writer who briefly worked for the Independent State of the Congo before penning *Heart of Darkness*, published in 1902

30-SECOND TEXT
Jeremy Rich

The inhabitants of what is today the Democratic Republic of the Congo were brutally exploited by Europeans seeking to get rich on the supply of rubber.

THE *SPIRIT OF ST. LOUIS*

the 30-second history

In 1919, wealthy hotel-owner
Raymond Orteig offered a prize of $25,000 to anyone who could fly from New York to Paris, an offer he renewed in 1926. Charles Lindbergh, a 25-year-old US Air Mail pilot, approached several aircraft manufacturers before B.F. "Frank" Mahoney, of Ryan Airlines, offered to build a plane for Lindbergh "at cost" ($10,580) capable of flying nonstop for 40 hours. The *Spirit of St. Louis*, named in honor of Lindbergh's financial backers from St. Louis, was a redesign of the Ryan M-2 mail plane, with longer wings to accommodate more fuel weight. Lindbergh made many of the specifications, including a single engine and main fuel tank placed in front of the pilot; Lindbergh feared being crushed between engine and fuel tank in the event of a crash. This meant that there was no forward visibility, save for an installed periscope. The pilot's seat was wicker, to reduce weight, and no parachute, radio, or navigation lights were on board. Lindbergh even cut the excess paper off his maps to reduce weight. On May 20, 1927, Lindbergh set off from Roosevelt Field on Long Island to land the next day in Paris. The feat set the stage for rapid transoceanic flights.

3-SECOND THRASH
Charles Lindbergh's solo transatlantic flight in the *Spirit of St. Louis* helped the public accept air travel as an exciting and viable means of transportation.

3-MINUTE THOUGHT
The *Spirit of St. Louis* made history before the transatlantic expedition when Lindbergh flew it from the factory in San Diego to New York City in 20 hours 21 minutes, a transcontinental record. After his New York–Paris flight, Lindbergh flew the *Spirit* across the US and to several Latin American countries, in a promotion of goodwill. Lindbergh donated the plane to the Smithsonian Institute in Washington, D.C., in 1928, where it is displayed today.

RELATED TOPICS
See also
SPUTNIK
page 24

ONE GIANT LEAP
page 148

3-SECOND BIOGRAPHIES
CHARLES AUGUSTUS
LINDBERGH
1902–74
American pilot who made the first solo nonstop flight across the Atlantic

RAYMOND ORTEIG
1870–1939
French-American hotelier whose prize sparked an era of aviation explosion in the years following Lindbergh's flight

30-SECOND TEXT
Laura J. Lee

Lindbergh and the Spirit of St. Louis won a place in history and on a US Air Mail stamp with the 3,600-mile (5,800km) New York–Paris flight.

THE HOLOCAUST

the 30-second history

Before the First World War the term genocide did not exist and holocaust generally referred to a large massacre. Both terms would become synonymous with Hitler and Nazi Germany's annihilation of European Jewry. The Holocaust was the state-sponsored, systematic persecution and murder of those considered a threat to the social, moral, economic, and political stability of Nazi Germany. Persecution began with anti-Semitic laws based on notions of scientific racism. In addition to Jews, Nazis targeted political opponents: the mentally and physically disabled; homosexuals; Jehovah's Witnesses; Catholics; and non-Aryans including Slavs, Roma, and Africans. Initially, mobile killing squads shot and buried victims en masse. Such methods proved inefficient and were replaced by concentration camps. Labor camps were established to work and starve prisoners to death. Death camps, however, were designed as efficient killing centers that deceived victims that they were being deloused by showers, only to be killed by Zyklon-B gas. The world was stunned by the base inhumanity of the camps. An estimated 11 million people died under the Nazis, of whom 6 million were Jews—almost 80 percent of the total European Jewish population.

RELATED TOPICS
See also
ADOLF HITLER
page 60

THE FIRST ARAB–ISRAELI WAR
page 64

3-SECOND THRASH
The Holocaust shocked the world and discredited notions of racism and Social Darwinism that had justified segregation and colonialism for many democracies.

3-MINUTE THOUGHT
Nations and citizens demanded moral, social, and political changes to ensure atrocities like the Holocaust would never be repeated. Deeper religious rapport between Jews and Christians developed as the need became evident to establish a Jewish homeland for survivors who could not return to their European communities. International tribunals were set up to ensure justice upon those who perpetrated crimes against humanity. The heightened awareness of the crime of genocide and international efforts to protect human rights reveal the lasting legacy of the Holocaust.

3-SECOND BIOGRAPHIES
HERMAN GOERING
1893–1946
German military leader who gave the direct order to Heydrich to formulate a plan for the "Final Solution"

HEINRICH HIMMLER
1900–45
German Nazi official who served as commander in chief of the concentration and death camps, and chief of the mobile death squads

REINHARD HEYDRICH
1904–42
German Nazi official who formulated and delivered the plan for the "Final Solution"

30-SECOND TEXT
Rita R. Thomas

The slogan Arbeit macht frei ("Work Makes You Free") taunted concentration camp inmates.

THE CULTURAL REVOLUTION

the 30-second history

Between 1966 and 1976 a radical
Maoist movement convulsed and reshaped
China. Dissatisfied with China's development, in
the mid-1960s communist leader Mao Zedong
regained his dominant status, resurrected
Maoism and promoted a Mao cult. The Great
Proletarian Cultural Revolution represented
Mao's attempt to implant his vision, destroy his
enemies, crush stifling bureaucracy, and renew
revolutionary vigor. Groups of militant workers
and students known as Red Guards attacked and
arrested anti-Mao leaders and smashed temples,
churches, and party and government
headquarters. Revolutionary committees led
by students, workers, and soldiers ran cities,
factories, and schools. The turmoil disrupted
industrial and agricultural production, closed
most schools for two years, and resulted in
thousands being killed, jailed, or removed from
office. Estimates of deaths range widely, from
500,000 to 3 million. Millions of others were sent
to remote areas to experience peasant life.
Anti-Mao officials, intellectuals, and people with
upper-class backgrounds faced public criticism
and often punishment. Soon even Mao was
dampening down the chaos. After his death in
1976 his successors shifted to less radical political
and economic policies. Nonetheless, the Cultural
Revolution legacy still influences Chinese life.

3-SECOND THRASH
This radical, decade-long,
movement in China
represented Mao Zedong's
attempt to transform
Chinese, politics, culture,
and economics while
revitalizing the revolution.

3-MINUTE THOUGHT
By disrupting daily life and
reshaping political, social,
economic, and cultural
institutions and ideology,
the Cultural Revolution
transformed China.
Individuals inspired by the
slogan "Serve the People"
subordinated their own
needs to the broader social
order. People—especially
villagers—shared resources:
food, draft animals, farm
equipment. Politicization of
the arts peaked. Red Guards
sang new songs praising
Mao. Militant operas and
ballets promoted
revolutionary values.
Chinese still debate the
value of these innovations.

RELATED TOPIC
See also
THE LONG MARCH
page 76

3-SECOND BIOGRAPHIES
MAO ZEDONG
1893–1976
Leader of Chinese Communist
Party and the first chairman of
the Peoples' Republic of China
between 1949–76

JIANG QING
1914–91
Mao's wife and a former movie
starlet who played a prominent
role in promoting and shaping
the Cultural Revolution

30-SECOND TEXT
Craig Lockard

*Red Guards carried
a little red book
containing short,
inspirational
quotations from
Mao's writings.*

DEATH IN DALLAS

the 30-second history

After narrowly winning the 1960 election, President John F. Kennedy knew he would need more than his television-debating persona to help him win again in 1964. On November 22, 1963 President and Mrs. Kennedy began a political fence-mending campaign in Dallas, Texas. At 12:30pm, three shots rang out. As Kennedy slumped into his wife's lap, the final shot exploded his head. The rapidity of the event was recorded in 26.6 seconds of 8mm film taken by Abraham Zapruder. Witnesses, however, provided confusing and conflicting stories of the tragic event. Fifty minutes after the confirmed newsflash of the president's death, Lee Harvey Oswald, an employee of the Texas School Book Depository, was arrested for shooting a Dallas policeman and as the prime suspect in the death of JFK. Unsure of the threat to national security, Vice-President Lyndon Johnson took the oath of office on board *Air Force One*, with Mrs. Kennedy by his side, still wearing her blood-stained clothes. For four days, the nation collectively mourned as all television networks provided constant coverage of funeral ceremonies. On the same day that Kennedy's funeral was held in Washington, D.C., Oswald was shot in the basement of the Dallas police station by nightclub owner Jack Ruby.

3-SECOND THRASH
The 1963 shooting of President John F. Kennedy shocked the world and helped set the stage for a decade of high-profile assassinations.

3-MINUTE THOUGHT
Kennedy's assassination was a shocking event that launched the concept of uninterrupted breaking news coverage to the American people; it also led to the people's distrust of their government. Before the publication of the Warren Commission, Americans believed Kennedy's death was a result of a conspiracy. Multiple conspiracy theories endure that propose as suspects Cuban President Fidel Castro, the Mafia, anti-Castro Cuban exiles, the KGB, the CIA, Hoover and the FBI, and even Lyndon Johnson.

RELATED TOPIC
See also
THE CUBAN MISSILE CRISIS
page 82

3-SECOND BIOGRAPHIES
ABRAHAM ZAPRUDER
1905–70
Dallas businessman who captured the clearest footage of the Kennedy assassination and was later called to testify before the Warren Commission

JACK RUBY
(JACOB LEON RUBENSTEIN)
1911–67
Dallas nightclub owner who killed suspect Lee Harvey Oswald as Kennedy's funeral was being broadcast to a live national audience

LEE HARVEY OSWALD
1939–63
Former US Marine, who, according to the Warren Commission, was the lone assassin of President John F. Kennedy

30-SECOND TEXT
Rita R. Thomas

Oswald fired his carbine from the sixth floor of the Book Depository building.

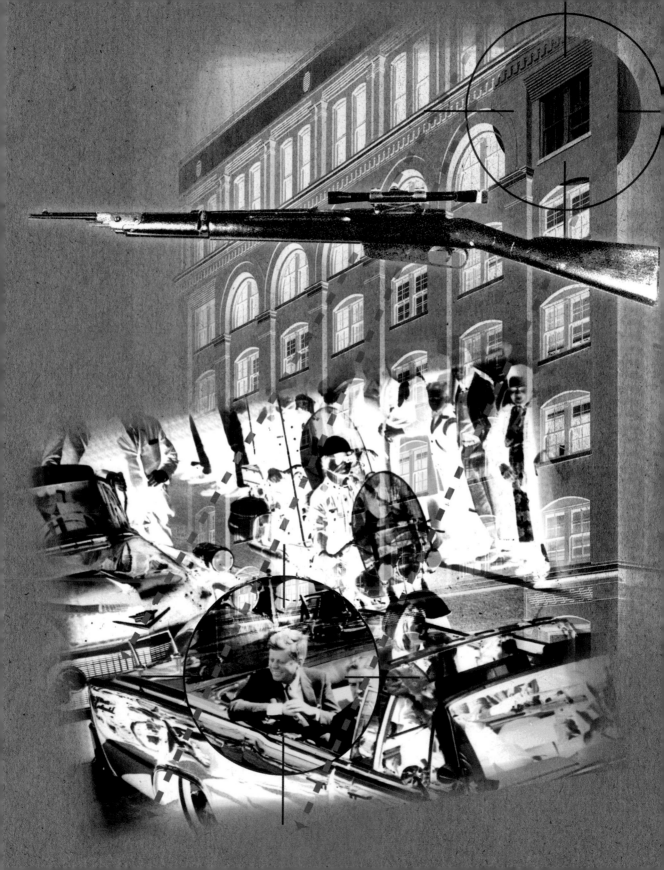

1885
Belgian king, Leopold II, claims Congo Free State as his personal property

1899
Joseph Conrad's *Heart of Darkness* published in serial form

1908
Colonial rule formally begins

July 2, 1925
Patrice Émery Lumumba born in the Kasai province of the central region of the Belgian Congo

1951
Weds Pauline Opangu in an arranged marriage

1955
Travels to Belgium for the first time

1958
Founds the Mouvement National Congolais (MNC)

1958
Meets Kwame Nkrumah, President of Ghana

1960
Elected prime minister, while in jail

1960
Congo gains indepence

January 17, 1961
Executed by firing squad

PATRICE LUMUMBA

One of the most important political assassination of the 20th century, the death of Patrice Lumumba, in 1961, played out most devastatingly for his native Congo, where a repeated series of disturbing, violent events have already lasted decades longer than Lumumba's brief political life.

Born Élias Okit'Asombo (meaning "heir of the cursed, who will die quickly"), Lumumba was the son of Tetela farmers in the mining province of Katanga (Kasai). He received a colonial education and training at the government post office training school. Lumumba became a postal worker and, later, an accountant, before marrying and turning to political life in the 1950s. An early African member of the Liberal Party, Lumumba traveled to Belgium and returned convinced that Africans could aspire to independence. He was arrested and imprisoned shortly upon his return.

In the late 1950s, Lumumba intensified his political engagement and repeatedly found himself in leadership roles. Helping to launch the anticolonial Mouvement national congolais (MNC) in 1958, he became the group's president. At the All-African Peoples Conference in Accra, Ghana, Lumumba represented the Congo. Ghana had just achieved independence in 1957, and Lumumba's contact with the new nation's president, Kwame Nkrumah, solidified his pan-Africanist beliefs and commitment to the struggle for independence at home.

Meanwhile, the United States and other nations in the West had begun to worry about the threat from outspoken African leaders, whose neutrality toward communism was held in suspicion during the height of the Cold War. The Belgians and Americans began to plot the eventual overthrow of Nkrumah (1966) and Lumumba's assassination (1961).

Decolonization only reinforced foreign domination and control over key mining and urban regions. At the Independence Day ceremony in 1960, the King Baudouin of Belgium's speech blithely celebrated the "genius" of the colonial past. Lumumba, the nation's first elected prime minister, did not shrink from pointing out the evils of colonialism and imperialism arguing that "it is too early to forget" the oppression, humiliation, torture, insults, maiming, and killings suffered by the colonized.

Briefly imprisoned, Lumumba feared for his life and the viability of autonomy in the face of excessive mining profits. He was captured by Belgian forces and executed in 1961. Between 1961 and the present, the Congo territory changed its official name a number of times, while still extracting the copper, gold, diamonds, gold, and cobalt (the so-called "conflict minerals") that power up the world's cell phones. Rather than silencing the past, Lumumba's martyrdom directed attention to the forces of capitalism, violence, and greed that continue to wreak havoc in the Congo.

Candice Goucher

"ONE GIANT LEAP"

the 30-second history

When President Kennedy gave his famous "Moon Speech" John Glenn had just become the first American to enter orbit, part of Project *Mercury*, NASA's endeavor to orbit Earth, determine whether man could function in space, and practice successfully recovering both man and spacecraft. *Gemini*'s mission was to observe man in space and prepare astronauts for long-duration flight and weightlessness, practicing reentry and landing, and testing docking methods and docked vehicles. NASA's most famous project, *Apollo*, was about getting to and exploring the Moon. On January 27, 1967 the first manned mission ended in tragedy during preflight testing: astronauts Virgil Grissom, Edward White, and Roger Chaffee were killed when fire erupted in the command module. *Apollo* flights 7–10 all launched successfully, running tests, orbiting Earth and the Moon, and testing equipment. It was time. Three men were aboard *Apollo 11*: Neil A. Armstrong, Michael Collins, and Edwin E. (Buzz) Aldrin, Jr. On July 20, 1969, seven years after the "Moon Speech," they announced, "Houston, Tranquility base here. The eagle has landed." Aldrin and Armstrong spent two and a half hours on the moon's surface. A further six *Apollo* missions followed, five of which successfully landed on the Moon.

RELATED TOPICS
See also
SPUTNIK
page 24

3-SECOND BIOGRAPHIES
JOHN GLENN
1921–
First American to orbit Earth (1962); former US senator

ALAN B. SHEPARD, JR.
1923–98
First American to enter space (1959); former United Nations delegate

NEIL A. ARMSTRONG
1930–2012
American astronaut and the first person to set foot on the moon (1969)

30-SECOND TEXT
Kristin Hornsby

3-SECOND THRASH
"One small step for [a] man, one giant leap for mankind."
Neil Armstrong

3-MINUTE THOUGHT
In 1957, the Soviets launched the first artificial satellite, *Sputnik 1*, into Earth's orbit, instigating the Space Race. Americans responded by launching their own satellite, *Explorer I* (1958), and created the National Aeronautics and Space Administration (NASA). The Soviets launched *Luna 2*, a space probe that landed on the Moon (1959), and sent cosmonaut Yuri Gagarin to orbit Earth (1961). The US responded with Project *Mercury*. When *Apollo 11* landed on the Moon, the US "won" the Space Race.

Buzz Aldrin takes small steps down from the lunar module Eagle then stands beside the US flag the crew planted on the Moon's surface.

0258 GMT

THE FALL OF THE BERLIN WALL

the 30-second history

3-SECOND THRASH
The fall of the Berlin Wall symbolized the end of the Cold War, which cost millions of lives and trillions of dollars.

3-MINUTE THOUGHT
The Cold War shaped world politics for most of the second half of the 20th century. While technically "cold" (there was rarely "hot" confrontation), power politics and fears drove surrogate wars, invasions, coups d'état, and arms races. By supplying arms the superpowers perverted nationalist movements, including the Korean War (1950–53), the Cuban missile crisis (1961–62), the Vietnam Conflict (1955–75), and Afghanistan (1979–89). Korea remains divided from the 1945 partition of communist North and capitalist South.

The Cold War was the conflict after the Second World War between the United States and the Soviet Union. The two superpowers engaged in an intense power struggle, reshaping the world into two hostile spheres of influence, divided by competing political and economic ideologies. Together with their military alliances—the North Atlantic Treaty Organization (NATO) and the Warsaw Pact—they launched a massive arms race that was fought bitterly around the globe, but refrained from direct armed conflict within Europe. The Berlin Wall, constructed in 1961, was a powerful symbol of this war, an "iron curtain" of concrete encircling a democratic West Berlin within communist East Germany. On November 9, 1989, ordinary men and women of Berlin breached the wall and began to tear it down brick by brick, in the wake of anticommunist revolutions sweeping across eastern Europe. This milestone initiated the process toward the German reunification of 1990, uniting two countries split since 1949, the German Democratic Republic (GDR—East), and the Federal Republic of Germany (FRG—West). The United States and the Soviet Union officially ended the Cold War with the Charter of Paris for New Europe (1990). The following year, the Soviet Union collapsed into 15 separate countries.

RELATED TOPICS
See also
THE FIRST ARAB–ISRAELI WAR
page 64

DIEN BIEN PHU
page 66

SOVIET DEFEAT IN AFGHANISTAN
page 68

THE CUBAN MISSILE CRISIS
page 82

3-SECOND BIOGRAPHIES
WINSTON CHURCHILL
1874–1965
British prime minister (1940–45, 1951–55) who coined the term "iron curtain" in March 1946

MIKHAIL GORBACHEV
1931–
Soviet Union's last president (1989–94), who introduced reforms such as perestroika and glasnost, which led to the eventual end of the Cold War

30-SECOND TEXT
Grace Chee

Berliners from east and west clambered up onto the wall to celebrate its demise.

APPENDICES

RESOURCES

BOOKS

Blackface, White Noise: Jewish Immigrants in the Hollywood Melting Pot
Michael Rogin
(University of California Press, 1998)

Bollywood: A Guidebook to Popular Hindi Cinema
Tejaswini Ganti
(Routledge, 2013)

A Briefer History of Time
Stephen Hawking and Leonard Mlodinow
(Bantam Press, 2008)

The Day the Bubble Burst: A Social History of the Wall Street Crash of 1929
Gordon Thomas and Max Morgan-Watts
(Doubleday & Company, 1979)

The Double Helix: A Personal Account of the Discovery of the Structure of DNA
James D. Watson
(Phoenix, 2010)

Hell in a Very Small Place: The Siege of Dien Bien Phu
Bernard Fall
(Da Capo Press, 2002)

Hip to the Trip: A Cultural History of Route 66
Peter B. Dedek
(University of New Mexico Press, 2007)

History In Three Keys: The Boxers as Event, Experience, and Myth
Paul A. Cohen
(Columbia University Press, 1998)

Hitler: A Biography
Ian Kershaw
(Penguin, 2001)

Magnificent Desolation: The Long Journey Home From the Moon
Buzz Aldrin
(Three Rivers Press, 2010)

Red Moon Rising: Sputnik and the Hidden Rivalries That Ignited the Space Age
Matthew Brzezinski
(Highbridge Company, 2007)

The Search for Modern China
Jonathan D. Spence
(W.W. Norton & Co., 2013)

Silenced Rivers: The Ecology and Politics of Large Dams
Patrick McCully
(Zed Books, 2001)

The Soviet–Afghan War: How a Superpower Fought and Lost
Lester W. Grau and Michael A. Gress
(University of Kansas, 2002)

Sputnik and the Soviet Space Challenge
Asif A. Siddiqi
(University Press of Florida, 2003)

Vietnam: A History
Stanley Karnow
(Pimlico, 1994)

World War One: A Layman's Guide
Scott Addington
(Createspace Independent Publishing, 2014)

Writing Jazz: Race, Nationalism, and Modern Culture in the 1920s
Nicholas M. Evans
(Routledge, 2000)

NOTES ON CONTRIBUTORS

EDITOR

Jonathan T. Reynolds is Professor of History at Northern Kentucky University, United States. He is a Fulbright Scholar, and received the Aggrey Award for Excellence in Teaching at Livingstone College and the Outstanding Junior Faculty award at NKU. He served on the Executive Board of the World History Association and Phi Alpha Theta. He is an editor for *H-Africa* and *World History Connected*. Reynolds teaches courses in African History, History of Imperialism, World History, the History of Food, and Historical Methodology.

Grace Chee is an Adjunct Assistant Professor of History at West Los Angeles College, and other LA Community Colleges, and serves on the executive board of the World History Association. Her publications include *Instructor's Manual: Worlds Together, Worlds Apart: A History of the World from the Beginnings of Humankind to the Present*, 4th edition, and *US Labor History Teaching Primer*.

Caryn Connelly is an Associate Professor of Spanish in the Department of World Languages and Literatures at Northern Kentucky University, where she teaches courses in Spanish language and Latin American literature and film. She holds a Master's degree in Spanish Linguistics from Arizona State University and a PhD in Hispanic and Luso-Brazilian Languages, Literatures, and Cultures from the University of Minnesota, Twin Cities.

Candice Goucher is Professor of History at Washington State University, Vancouver, and Trent R. Dames Civil Engineering History Fellow at the Huntington Library, California. Trained as an archaeologist, Candice has conducted excavations in the Caribbean and West Africa, and has coauthored world history textbooks, including the 2nd edition of *World History: Journeys from Past to Present* and was colead scholar on the Annenberg/Corporation for Public Broadcasting multimedia project *Bridging World History*.

Cary D. Harlow is a freelance writer and editor with a degree in Broadcast Journalism from the University of Cincinnati. He also works for the Hewlett Packard Company as a Global Education Services Lead and Director of Corporate Education. He has previously worked as a news producer with CNN, a film/video director in corporate communications for Procter & Gamble, and is also regular contributor and presenter for the Learning Consortium.

Kristin Hornsby is a playwright and lecturer; she teaches theater and film-based courses in the Northern Kentucky University Honors Program. She earned an MFA in Stage and Screenwriting from Florida State University. Kristin's plays have been read and produced in Florida, Kentucky, and New York, and several of her screenplays have been made into short films. Her writing credits include *twentysomething*, *The Boy Who Knew Too Much*, and *When the Dealing's Done*. Kristin is an associate member of the Dramatists Guild of America.

Laura J. Lee is a doctoral candidate in Educational Psychology at the University of Memphis. Her research interests include narrative inquiry, gifted and twice-exceptional education, cooperative learning, and gender development. She has taught from preschool to university level, and currently teaches a Lifespan Development course to pre-service teachers. She holds BS and MS degrees in Psychology and has worked in personnel research for the US Navy.

Craig A. Lockard is Ben and Joyce Rosenberg Professor of History Emeritus at the University of Wisconsin-Green Bay. His publications include *Southeast Asia in World History* and *Dance of Life: Popular Music and Politics in Southeast Asia*. Professor Lockard has served on the editorial boards of the *Journal of World History*, *World History Connected*, *The History Teacher*, and the *Journal of Asian Studies*.

Sara Patenaude is a doctoral candidate in history at Georgia State University and an Urban Fellow with the Center for the Study of Metropolitan Growth. Her research interests include the histories of city planning, social justice, and public policy. She has worked in several museums, including the Cincinnati History Center, the National Electronics Museum, and the Jewish Museum of Maryland.

Jeremy Rich is an Associate Professor of History at Marywood University in Scranton, Pennsylvania. He is a specialist in central African history, and has written two books: *A Workman is Worthy of His Meat: Food and Colonialism in the Gabon Estuary* and *Missing Links: The African and American Worlds of R.L. Garner, Primate Collector*. He has also published numerous articles on the history of Gabon and the Democratic Republic of Congo.

Timothy D. Sofranko is an award-winning Senior Photographer for Northern Kentucky University. He previously investigated the issues leading to Chinese illegal immigration to the US Territories in the Pacific Islands, and the impact of Mexican immigration on the public school system in southern California. His work has been published in the *New York Times*, the *New York Post*, and *USA Today*. He earned his Master of Fine Arts from the State University of New York at New Paltz.

Kristopher Teters is a Lecturer at Northern Kentucky University, where he teaches courses on American history. He specializes in 19th-century America. His manuscript on emancipation and the Union army in the western theater is currently under contract with the University of North Carolina Press. Kris has written several articles on a variety of topics related to the Civil War period. He holds a PhD in history from the University of Alabama.

Rita R. Thomas is an adjunct instructor of History at Maysville Community and Technical College, in Maysville, Kentucky. In 2009 Ms. Thomas received her MSc in Slavery and Forced Labour Studies from the University of Edinburgh. She is currently serving as the Executive Director, the Ohio River National Freedom Corridor and as the Vice President of the Bracken County, Kentucky Historical Society.

Russell Zimmerman is a lecturer in History at Tarleton State University, Texas. He was the recipient of the W. Frank Steely award from the History and Geography Department at Northern Kentucky University and the Flora H. Floust Scholarship for Academic Excellence at Tarleton State University. Russell is also a popular author of other-than-academic materials, and has been a prolific contributor to alternate history, wargaming, role-playing games, and science fiction libraries.

INDEX

ACKNOWLEDGMENTS

AUTHOR ACKNOWLEDGMENTS
First off, thanks to Jamie Pumfrey, Stephanie Evans, and Caroline Earle of Ivy Press for being such a great editorial team to collaborate with. It's the real pros who know how to make it work but keep it fun at the same time. A hat tip goes to Professor Ross Dunn for putting me in touch with Ivy. I'd also like to thank all of the contributors to this volume. Each and every one were a pleasure to work with, and I appreciate the thought, expertise, and creativity each of you brought to the project. At Northern Kentucky University I'd like to thank my cool Department Chair William Landon for his unfailing support, and Professors Jim Ramage, Bob Vitz, and Jeffrey Williams for their mentorship and encouragement over the years. Thanks also to a host of great colleagues and students who have insured that my job never feels like work. And, if I may fire up the Wayback Machine, thanks to Professors Rosalind Hackett, Cynthia Fleming, and James Farr for encouraging me to pursue an academic career. I've never forgotten it. And, as always, I want to thank my dear wife, Dr. Ngozi Victoria Uti for her support and our children William and Ojie for their patience while Dad finished up yet another book!